LESSONS
FROM THE TOP

TOP

What I've Learned About
Winning and Leading

KEN SMITH

Dedication

I've been taught that when someone helps me as many of you have done in the writing of this book, I should sit down and write thank-you notes or "hug your necks." I will do that, but I also want to put my thanks in print. Consider this as a note and a big hug to all of you who have made such a difference in my life. Special thanks to:

- Donnelle, who is always there for me.
- Richard and Karen, my children, who turned me loose to research this material when I should have been spending time with them.
- Steve Brown, who has always been my mentor.
- Steve Cloud, Charles Roesel, and Don Pratt, who were my pastors during the years that I compiled all this material.
- Dennis Rogers, who prays for me faithfully on the journey.
- Bobby Bowden, who let me serve as chaplain for his team and who remains my friend.
- Countless church members, who just let me do my own thing.
- A host of high school coaches, who are at the top, even if no one knows it: Brad Lane, Jimmy Scroggins, Mickey Lindsey, Ron Chambers, and others.
- The Board of Ken Smith Ministries, Inc., who are my friends and partners on my journey.
  and especially
- Bobbie McAdams, who spent hours working on the book and sharing her expertise.

Hugs and thanks to all of you.

Ken Smith

Leadership Definitions from Some Leaders at the Top

"I believe a leader is someone who is willing to serve those that God has put him in authority over. He needs to have a clear vision and the ability to communicate it to those around him and to get them motivated to move toward their ultimate goal. He needs to be willing to sacrifice his life for the betterment of the group." -Mark Richt, Head Football Coach, University of Georgia

"A leader has the ability to make people around him better by showing a genuine concern for them and their role in his organization." -Brad Scott, Assistant Head Football Coach, Clemson University

"A true leader has the ability to gain respect and give respect. A leader has the self-motivation and positive outlook on life for which others thirst. The leadership that lasts is not self-centered but team (group) centered. The great leaders are those that are not afraid of failure. This world cries out for LEADERS." -Mike Turner, Assistant Football Coach/Offensive Coordinator, Carson Newman College

"A leader is one who understands what his role is; one who listens; one who is a person of character and integrity; and one who can follow direction and who wants to lead." -Ken Rucker, Assistant Coach/Running Backs, University of Texas

"A leader, in the strictest sense, is someone others follow. Of course, we have to parse that definition carefully. Some leaders, for instance, don't necessarily have a following all the time. Winston Churchill during the nineteen-thirties is an example. Very few paid attention to his warnings about Nazi Germany during those years, and it was only when Great Britain came under attack by Hitler's regime that Churchill's value was recognized. Then, a whole nation, belatedly recognizing the accuracy of his perspectives as well as the passion of his convictions, followed him. Leaders, then, are gifted people who are sure enough of their causes, of their directions, to maintain their courses through those times when others don't see things quite the same way, as did

Churchill. We can further narrow down the definition by saying at some point, leaders must be able to look behind them and see followers who are willing to accept them in that position. Leadership is not a technique that can be learned, although techniques are important. Neither is leadership a set of guidelines that must be followed, a 1-2-3 rulebook for success. It's instead an alchemist's brew that mixes personality with passion and circumstances to yield the philosopher's stone. The end result of leadership is a nation or system or organization or team or church accomplishing goals that otherwise could not be imagined." -Mike Turner, Pastor, First Baptist Church, Jacksonville, North Carolina

"A leader is someone who takes another person or group of people to a place they could not go alone; or achieve a goal they could not achieve alone. The best leaders I have known have been those that inspired others by their servanthood. You cannot truly lead another person without serving them." -Dean Hood, Defensive Coordinator/Secondary, Wake Forest University

"A leader is one who has the vision and passion to take an individual or team to a place they cannot take themselves. Leadership is about relationships and the ability to focus on people that are working beside you to accomplish the goals for which you are striving. It is the quality to make someone see his (her) worth, value and significance as a child of God which will enable him (her) to take his (her) talents to another level of achievement. Leadership is character because there must be tremendous trust among the members of the team in the man who is leading them to accomplish the victory they all desire. Finally, the successful leader lives by this statement: "No one cares how much you know until they know how much you care." -Richard Bell, Defensive Coordinator/Inside Linebacker Coach, Air Force Academy

In preparation for the writing of this book, I asked several people for their validation of my ability to help others benefit from lessons I've learned from being around people at the top. Here are some of their responses:

"Ken Smith relates to high school and college athletes as well or better than anyone I know in regard to Christ. His enthusiasm for Jesus jumps out at you. Many an athlete at FSU changed his life around due to his association with Ken." -Bobby Bowden, Head Football Coach, Florida State University

"The Lord has blessed Ken Smith with the gift to motivate and inspire every age group to take their God-given abilities to a higher level for his glory. I believe Ken is truly one of the outstanding motivational speakers of our time." -Richard Bell, Defensive Coordinator/Inside Linebacker Coach, Air Force Academy

"If Ken Smith writes a book on leadership I am going to read it because #1 it is going to be funny, #2 it is going to be creative, and most importantly #3 it is going to have its foundation in Biblical truth!" -Dean Hood, Defensive Coordinator/Secondary, Wake Forest University

"Ken Smith has been around enough great leaders to know what makes them tick. I recommend this book to anyone who has ever wondered what it takes to be a winner at the game of life." -Mike Turner, Pastor, First Baptist Church, Jacksonville, North Carolina

"Ken Smith is capable of writing this book because he is a man of integrity, a man of character, a man of GOD, and a leader of men for a long time." -Ken Rucker, Assistant Coach/Running Backs, University of Texas

"Ken Smith has had the experiences most (people) have not had. He has insights that few have. The combination means −I need this book."-Ken Sparks, Head Football Coach, Carson Newman College

"When Ken Smith writes I read and learn." -Dal Shealy, President, Fellowship of Christian Athletes

"Ken Smith's love of people, his family and our Master Coach makes him one of the nation's most outstanding leaders. He leads all in the 'right' direction." -Fisher DeBerry, Head Football Coach, Air Force Academy

"Whenever Ken Smith writes a book, I want to read it! Ken has been blessed in the unique way that he delivers his message. At Carson Newman College we think Ken Smith is 'the best there ever was!'" -Mike Turner, Assistant Football Coach/Offensive Coordinator, Carson Newman College

"I have known Ken Smith for nearly twenty years. I know what kind of leader he is, and I know the leaders he has been around, so he certainly knows one when he sees one. He has a great ability to communicate all the things that he has learned over the years." -Mark Richt, Head Football Coach, University of Georgia

"Ken Smith is a leader who writes from his personal experience. He understands what it takes to be one and, like a weight lifter pressing to get stronger every day, Ken presses forward daily developing his leadership skills. The best part about Ken is that he has a heart for leaders." -Jim Ramsey, Pastor, First Baptist Church, Thomson, Georgia

"I have known Ken Smith for over twenty years. He has served as my pastor and the chaplain of football teams that I have coached. He is a proven leader whose unique ability to communicate through storytelling and humor will captivate you as he shares the simple truths about winning and leading. Simply put, he is a special man with a special message." -Brad Scott, Assistant Head Football Coach, Clemson University

"Ken Smith combines an assortment of experiences and acquaintances with his tremendous sense of humor to bless me, and others, in a way that transcends gender, race, creed and color impacting all ages of society for good." -Bob Sanders, Defensive Assistant Coach, Green Bay Packers

"After many years, Ken Smith has been around some of the best coaches in college athletics and seen it all. His ability to put these experiences into words is a <u>must read</u> for anyone interested in the athletic arena. I think this book would benefit the athlete, the coach, the father, the husband, or those in managerial positions. In any walk of life, this book covers it all. -Tommy Bowden, Head Football Coach, Clemson University

Introduction

I do not know why it has happened to me, but I have led a life that has put me in contact with successful people in various fields. While preaching in preparation for the Billy Graham Evangelistic Association on several occasions, I have become a part of one of the greatest ministries in Christian history. I have spoken and counseled for several years to a most exciting multilevel business. I have stood on the sidelines with the coach who has the most wins in college football history, Bobby Bowden. I have also worked with other great football coaches, such as Carson Newman College's head football coach Ken Sparks, who has won five national championships, Tommy Bowden, 2003 Coach of the Year in the Atlantic Coast Conference, Chuck Amato, head coach at North Carolina State University, Mark Richt, head coach at the University of Georgia, Jackie Sherrill, former head coach at Mississippi State University, and Fisher DeBerry, head coach at the Air Force Academy. I should also mention working with the late Nick Hyder, one of the most successful high school coaches in America at Valdosta, Georgia. I have even served on boards with the late Tom Landry, former coach of the Dallas Cowboys, Grant Teaff, director of the College Football Association, and Tom Osborne, former head coach at the University of Nebraska.

I have served as team chaplain for Florida State University and the University of South Carolina, as well as the Director of Player Relations at Mississippi State University. I have conducted chapel services for college teams, high school teams, and professional football teams such as the Indianapolis Colts, Tampa Bay Buccaneers, Chicago Bears, and Miami Dolphins.

I tell this not so I can boast of my achievements, but to illustrate how through God's blessings I have walked in the shadows of some of the greatest leaders in this generation. I have tried to learn by studying and observing leadership and personality styles to see if any consistent conclusions might be drawn.

I would in no way impugn the names of these leaders or share too many secret insights of their techniques and styles. I want them all to know that I appreciate the opportunity to know

1

and work with them, and that I treasure every event and every conversation that I have had with each of them. Thanks for the memories.

As I have said, I have watched and learned some of the strategies that have made them so successful, and I have written this book in the hope that I might help you use some of the same techniques to become a better leader and a winner for the rest of your life. In short, I hope you can learn some of the things that I have learned in the shadow of these great leaders. I do not claim to be an expert or authority on what I am sharing, but I am a better man for having walked in their shadows. I am indebted to those leaders for what I have learned and observed. Now I wish to share my recollections with you in the hope that you may enhance your journey.

GOOD READING! GROW! OUR WORLD NEEDS MORE WINNERS!

My Definition of Success:

Success is never a good measurement of life because so many definitions change according to circumstances. I figure what you really want out of life is to get to the point where you can say, "I like being who I am and doing what I do. I think I am making a difference, and I seem to be more blessed than when I started!"

Chapter 1
The Best I Have Ever Seen

"Teach your children to choose the right path, and when they are older, they will remain upon it." -Proverbs 22:6 (NLT)

"A good leader inspires other people with confidence in the leader; a great leader inspires them with confidence in themselves." -Unknown

"I feel some leaders are born but most of them are self trained. You can train to be a leader. First you need the desire to want to lead. Be sure you choose to lead in a positive way with high moral standards. If you're an athlete, politician, coach, or military officer, you'll lead whether you wish to or not —good or bad. Who is a leader? He is someone people will follow."-Bobby Bowden, Head Football Coach, Florida State University

Certainly, we in this country have defined greatness as **winning**. I suppose in some ways that is true, but if true, I question Alabama's Coach Bear Bryant's infatuation with the "junction boys." The "junction boys" were a group of young athletes from Texas A & M University that Coach Bryant took to Junction, a west Texas town, for extra work when he first went to Texas A & M as head coach. They spent the preseason practice under tough circumstances. They practiced hard, gave their all, but failed to have a winning season. However, they became the basis for Bryant's great football program at Texas A & M. Winning with that group did not signify greatness; effort did!

I also question other cases when the best people have not been rewarded for their efforts. I question why the greatest athlete whom I have ever coached never made it to the big leagues. I question why great church leaders have never been recognized by their peers or the leaders of their denominations. I question why outstanding coaches at small schools never seem to win awards. I question why corporate America does not always promote the most deserving individual. Obviously, receiving awards or promotions alone does not signify greatness. Is greatness definable in worldly terms, or is it simply experienced by leaders and the people who follow them?

In 1965-67, I worked with the best basketball team I have ever seen. I recall several games that stand out in my mind, especially that final victory in the first season. No one expected the team to win. The newspapers and other coaches claimed that the players were outclassed and possessed far less talent than the competition. However, the attitude of each player, when he arrived at the game site, indicated his intention. The team felt it could not fail because each player:

- Had worked too hard.
- Had practiced too long.
- Had studied too hard.
- Had prepared to the last detail.

It didn't matter what someone else thought or said. Each and every player had come to win. The circumstances surrounding the game were intimidating to say the least:

- The crowd was against them.
- The team had made a long trip.
- The team entered the game with little rest.
- The surroundings were hostile.
- The opportunity was demanding!

No one on that team had come to the game to go home second. From the opening whistle to the last, each player gave every ounce of his energy to achieve the victory. No one left anything on the court of combat. Each gave his all! The team won!

On the long trip home, I remember relishing the outcome and celebrating what seemed an unbelievable victory with the team. But as I relished the win, I asked myself "how?" How had this outmanned, under-talented team "pulled-it-off"? How had they as a team done it? How had they won a victory and started a tradition that would carry on for the rest of their lives?

I suppose these thoughts have permeated all my learning about leadership, and that event gave me the first idea for this book. That team had put into practice all the elements that take a team from good to great! These young men with the proper leadership had taken the game to another level. **They were the best I had ever seen because they acted on a vision. They had a dream.**

Whatever else you say about leadership you have to start with a basic assumption: Leadership is taking someone (or some team) from point A to point B. According to most people, a leader gets people to accomplish a specific purpose. However, to move people in any direction, someone must sell a vision, a dream.

For years I have observed that great teams in athletics, great teams in churches, and great teams in sales all have a **buy-in** time. At some point the team must see the vision, buy the dream, and head off in that direction. Every coach who has won, every pastor who has kept his church from stagnating, every sales leader who has an outstanding sales team knows and can recall the moment that the buy-in occurred.

Do you recall the movie *Remember the Titans*? In it the actor Denzel Washington plays a coach from Virginia who has worked hard to get his racially divided team together, but he hasn't accomplished his goal. An argument in a Civil War Battlefield Park causes the two groups to buy-into the dream of becoming a team.

Buy-ins can occur anywhere and at any time. I have seen the buy-in occur in an August practice, at a late-night sales meeting, and at an early morning Bible study.

If you decide to become a leader, you start with the buy-in before you can do anything else. This buy-in takes every people skill you have learned and every teaching skill you possess. It requires a block of time devoted to building relationships so that the group or team accepts the buy-in.

When the buy-in occurs, leadership has a running head start. Michael Barrett, a friend and a successful pastor from North Carolina, explains that when it comes to putting together a team to build a new church or any other important undertaking, he hires people that have the same passion that he has. He says, "If their passion is kin to my passion, I can train them to do their job."

I have studied the buy-in from every angle. It can be found in a winning tradition. Coaching was easy for me as a young man

5

at Starkville High School in Mississippi because the school had a winning tradition. The athletes thought they were supposed to win so selling the buy-in was easy. Another example of an established tradition is the late Nick Hyder's program at Valdosta High School in Georgia. He had a head start because former coach, Wright Bazemore, had already established a winning program there.

But what of the athletic team, the church group, or the sales team where no tradition exists. How do you accomplish the buy-in? Several ways, beginning with **truth and caring**, come to mind.

So often people think if they hype something enough, or if they promote it enough, others will eventually buy it. That can work, but leveling with people accomplishes the buy-in in a far better way. For instance, a large company promoted a very bright young salesman as one of its district sales managers. In his new job, he had to manage several people who had more experience and more longevity in the territory than he. At his team's first meeting he simply told them, "I don't make money if you don't. I don't succeed if you don't. So understand that although I may make mistakes in this process, you will never have to question whether I make decisions with you in mind or not." He had told them the **truth** about his position and had begun to build bridges.

That same district manager made a science of discovering the behavior styles and the likes and dislikes of each of his team members. He learned about their families, their dreams, and their desires. He invested in them as individuals. After being with the company for only a short time that young man received an award for leading the outstanding sales team in his company. Several of his peers presented him with a plaque for his leadership, which simply stated, "**Thank you for teaching us that people don't care what you know until they know that you care.**" For him **caring** was an investment in his team.

For you to succeed in creating a winning attitude with your people, you must be **involved in their endeavors**. The long road trips, the coffee breaks, the walking into the locker room for a brief visit, the invitation to your home, the card you write, or the call you make, all show that you care. This interest in each person on the team builds that winning attitude within the team, which can then lead to a winning tradition.

Coach Dan Redding of Carson Newman College worked on and off the field with my son Richard. I am certain that his caring helped Richard, not only with the skills needed for playing football but also with the skills needed for living life well. Dan's caring enabled Richard to have successful years as a wide receiver for the team while he completed his degree. That caring showed him the type of person he wants to be in life.

Not only must you show that you care, you must also **teach with a purpose.** To be a good leader you must dispense worthwhile information to your teams as the final part of the buy-in process. Keeping people informed about the best techniques and the important facts that will help them do their jobs better is essential. In the corporate world, in the church world, and in the sports arena you need to assimilate information so that people can know what constitutes good and necessary information as opposed to unnecessary or bad information and the difference between the two.

In churches, as well as on athletic or business teams, you must keep people informed about the ultimate goal. Gary Redding, Pastor at First Baptist Church, North Augusta, South Carolina, has town hall meetings where he sits on a stool before his congregation and lets the members ask questions whenever the church is facing a major issue that could be divisive. His long tenure indicates that his information sharing is solid.

You must have a **determination to make your goal happen.** It never happens without concentrated effort and time. Work is hard! You must have a great desire to obtain a certain goal and the determination to utilize your abilities to reach that goal.

As we made the trip home after the great win in 1965, I realized that the reason the victory had occurred was the understanding of the price. Each player had experienced the buy-in. As a result of the buy-in, he had realized the price he had to pay to see the vision come true. I saw these guys work as hard as any group of players that I have ever seen. Each player worked on cold days and hot days, under good conditions and under bad ones. The players, like members of all teams, complained and growled, but the buy-in had occurred; therefore, the work was a given.

The key word is responsibility. ***Responsibility*** by definition means "answerable or accountable for." For what are you responsible? You are responsible for everything you think, say, or do. Why? Because no matter what or whom you can blame for the circumstances of your life, you are still answerable for the consequences of your actions. People too often in this country try to place blame for their actions on others or upon fate. However, until every person fully realizes that each is totally responsible for his or her own life, society, as a whole, shall operate under a false and distorted assumption of what responsibility means. You as a leader must accept responsibility for all you think, say, or do and teach those you lead to do the same!

Rising above one's environment or circumstances is another trait of a true winner. Ted Engstrom, President Emeritus of World Vision International, spoke this way about people who literally used their circumstances:

Cripple him, and you have a Sir Walter Scott. Lock him in a prison cell, and you have a John Bunyan. Bury him in the snows of Valley Forge, and you have a George Washington. Raise him in abject poverty and you have an Abraham Lincoln. Strike him down with infantile paralysis, and he becomes Franklin Roosevelt. Burn him so severely that the doctors say he'll never walk again, and you have a Glenn Cunningham (set the world's one mile record in 1934). Deafen him and you have a Ludwig van Beethoven. Have him or her born black in a society filled with racial discrimination and you have a Booker T. Washington, a Marian Anderson, or a George Washington Carver. Call him a slow learner, 'retarded' and write him off as uneducable, and you have an Albert Einstein. As one man summed it up: Life is about 20% in what happens to us and 80% in the way we respond to the events.

Winners and leaders determine their own system for deciding how to treat any given situation. Therefore, you must make a decision to pay whatever price to achieve and **establish your own system**. Bobby Bowden has done this at Florida State University and Mark Richt is beginning the process at the

8

University of Georgia. I have seen pastors, like Tom Smiley of Lakeview Baptist Church, Gainesville, Georgia, and Charles Roesel at First Baptist Church, Leesburg, Florida, refuse to accept anyone else's system. Instead each has decided, under a really strong desire to honor his calling, to create and operate his own system.

I am stunned by how many of you reading this book have been duped into buying into other peoples' systems and then have been having horrific problems trying to accommodate your behavior style and your talents to their way of doing things. Create your own system which fits your own personality and style.

The late Findley Edge, a former professor at Southern Seminary, greatly influenced me. Dr. Edge talked about every person finding what he called his or her "Eureka," the place that defines who you are and what you do. Each person should function in that place where he or she becomes alive. Once you find it, you will discover personal peace and satisfaction.

You must become personally responsible for where you are headed. You can do this by creating your own way of doing things and accepting the responsibility for that system. This responsibility creates your work ethic.

If you have experienced the buy-in, you are now ready to be personally responsible for the vision to come true. The running, the working, the learning, and the practicing are all part of your accepting responsibility for the vision. You will run sprints, make visits, or learn techniques for whatever the situation or setting demands.

When Jim Tressel's Ohio State's Buckeyes won the National Championship game in 2003, a Buckeye fan, wrote a speech suggesting what he believed Coach Tressel should say to the team before the game. The "pre-game" speech contained all the elements of the dream that the team had bought into months before that important game. On that day the buy-in had to be completed. The fan began the imaginary meeting with a speech telling the players that they had begun a journey twelve months earlier when each of them had bought into the dream of becoming the national champions. After the buy-in had occurred, each had committed himself to giving all that was required to obtain that goal. Everyone had practiced hard and had sacrificed much to reach the threshold of their goal. He told them the time had come to savor their accomplishments, but the time had also come to use all the skills that they had learned to reach the final goal. It was time to complete the dream!

Let me return to that basketball team that no one expected to win. Those players were also winners, not on a national front, but winners nevertheless. On that long trip home after that wondrous final victory of the 1965 season, I realized that each player had bought a dream and had begun the winning ways long before the games themselves had begun. This team had developed a third quality as well. This quality contained the key to their winning. This team's work ethic, expectation, and sense of pride became central parts of its behavior. This team brought to mind that great Pittsburgh Pirate baseball team that adopted the song, "We Are Family." That is what those guys had become. They had become a family. They had pushed each other during practice and demanded the proper behavior in the classroom. They had stayed together, had worked together, and had laughed together as only a family would. I saw them, from the very first day of practice; hold each other accountable for the best performance possible. Not many pep talks from the coach were needed because they encouraged each other. This team can be used as an example for what you need to do to create a winning team or group. Create within your team or group this **feeling of family.**

Over the years I have been chaplain for three football teams and have conducted chapel services for the National Football League, for colleges, and for high school teams. The one thing I have tried to get across to each of these groups is that every time the players take the field, they make a choice about what they want and how they will go about getting it.

One of the most exciting visits I make each year is to the Air Force Academy. I was privileged to give the following devotion, "Becoming a Team of Character: The Choice," to this awesome group of young people and their coaches on Friday night before they were to play California. Joshua is speaking to the Israelites telling them what God has said:

> *[11]"When you crossed the Jordan River and came to Jericho, the men of Jericho fought against you. There were also many others who fought you,*

including the Amorites, the Perizzites, the Canaanites, the Hittites, the Girgashites, the Hivites, and the Jebusites. But I gave you victory over them. [12]And I sent hornets ahead of you to drive out the two kings of the Amorites. It was not your swords or bows that brought you victory. [13]I gave you land you had not worked for, and I gave you cities you did not build—the cities in which you are now living. I gave you vineyards and olive groves for food, though you did not plant them."

[14]"So honor the LORD and serve him wholeheartedly. Put away forever the idols your ancestors worshiped when they lived beyond the Euphrates River and in Egypt. Serve the LORD alone. [15]But if you are unwilling to serve the LORD, then choose today whom you will serve. Would you prefer the gods your ancestors served beyond the Euphrates? Or will it be the gods of the Amorites in whose land you now live? But as for me and my family, we will serve the LORD."

[16]The people replied, "We would never forsake the LORD and worship other gods. [17]For the LORD our God is the one who rescued us and our ancestors from slavery in the land of Egypt. He performed mighty miracles before our very eyes. As we traveled through the wilderness among our enemies, he preserved us. [18]It was the LORD who drove out the Amorites and the other nations living here in the land. So we, too, will serve the LORD, for he alone is our God."

[19]Then Joshua said to the people, "You are not able to serve the LORD, for he is a holy and jealous God. He will not forgive your rebellion and sins. [20]If you forsake the LORD and serve other gods, he will turn against you and destroy you, even though he has been so good to you."

[21]But the people answered Joshua, saying, "No, we are determined to serve the LORD!"

*[22]"You are accountable for this decision,"
Joshua said, "You have chosen to serve the LORD."*

"Yes," they replied, "we are accountable."

*[23]"All right then," Joshua said, "destroy the
idols among you, and turn your hearts to the Lord,
the God of Israel."*

*[24]The people said to Joshua, "We will serve
the Lord our God. We will obey him alone."*

*[25]So Joshua made a covenant with
the people that day at Shechem, committing them to
a permanent and binding contract between
themselves and the LORD.* -Joshua 24:11-25 (NLT)

The Israelites had found the days both new
and exciting. They had reached the outskirts of the
land that God had given them. The future lay before
them. The opportunity seemed great. However,
Joshua wanted to make a point. He wanted them to
understand that they would have to **pay for the
opportunity**. He reminded them that times would
come when they might want to quit. Times might
come when they would wish to turn back. He told
them that they would have to pay in some manner
for the opportunity.

The crowds, looking at the opportunity,
stood at the crossroads and wondered what to do.
They realized that their dreams lay before them.
They would have every opportunity to advance, but
they had to make a choice about some things. They
had to **choose** that day what they wanted to do. I
once heard a pastor say that the more he learned of
Joshua the more he liked him. The man was a
leader! He demanded that the Israelites make a
choice and stand firm. They could not waver.
Joshua said that he had chosen. He was not turning
back. They had to choose and understand that the
choice would have a price that must be paid.

Gentlemen, I don't always know about
football, but I know that in order for a team to have

a good year, its players must make a definitive choice and stand by that choice.

This story of Joshua is as much like this game as I can find in the Scripture. Today you must decide some things. This coaching staff cannot make the choice. The fans who buy tickets cannot make the choice. The television critics who say you are not any good cannot make the choice. The day has arrived when you must choose.

Some players have already chosen. They did some unwise things and are no longer here. They decided that the team and this opportunity did not mean anything to them. They wanted to do some things their way instead of the way the coaches required; therefore, they had to leave.

Now please, hear me. You are standing on the edge of a great year. The time has come to choose.

You must go to the task as Joshua did and say, 'Me and my house ... we have chosen!' You must make the choice and be willing to stand on it.

You do not make the choice alone. The group must choose. Men look around this room. You have worked too hard this year not to take advantage of the opportunity presented to you. You have sweated in the weight room and have run during the spring and the off-season. You have achieved too much not to encourage each other to make this happen.

It will **cost** you. When the Israelites reached the river, Joshua realized what lay before them. They would face battles and entrenched enemies, but they had an enormous possibility. He wanted them to decide if it was worth it. Did they really want to occupy the land that was in front of them? Did they want to pay the price?

Welcome to where you are. You have to decide. You have to decide as a group, and you have to make up your mind as an individual if you want to pay the price. You will pay the price with your bodies. Play with courage. Play with boldness. The cost is high, but unless you are willing to pay it, you will lose it all.

You have reached decision time, pure and simple. With the proper choice, you take the field and make it happen, or the year becomes a total waste.

Notice that the price starts with an individual commitment. Have you chosen? I don't care where you are or what position team you are on; have you made the decision to make something happen? Have you decided that you will accomplish your job so well that you will have no doubt? Will you handle your assignment within yourself? If so, you have made a choice.

Have you heard of the story of the raid a group of soldiers made on an island? As the troops left their boats, they looked back to see their captain burning their boats. There was no turning back for the soldiers that day. Let's burn the boats and head toward the victory.

To accomplish your goal:
- Talk with each other.
- Encourage each other.
- Push each other.
- Help each other.
- Stretch each other.
- Make this deal.

All of you matter: the guy who will watch all year, the scouting team, the kicking team, and the starting team. Choose to make this the best year of your life!

Guys, you have an opportunity to be an exciting team, but you will not do it as individuals. Every man here has to step up and make it happen. You must choose this day whom you will serve, and what you want to do. Before this day is over, each of you must choose!

The winning attitude taught in that speech should foster the type of passion that you as a leader must inspire in each member of your team, whether the team is a sporting team, a business team, or a church team. You must elicit the best effort that each of your team members can give toward the team's goal.

The attitude taught in that speech also calls forth the dedication toward winning that each of the members of that extraordinary team of 1965 possessed. On that trip home after the final game of the 1965 season as I listened to the athletes' conversation, I became acutely aware that they had bought a vision, had taken responsibility, had become a "family" team, and had chosen to pay the price for that dream. Those guys on the trip home from that unbelievable win were always in a process of becoming. They had worked at being the best. This win would not be the end. They had met what many called a superior foe. They had beaten that foe with a team effort. A sense of pride permeated this team that night. I knew it was going to be fun to watch them as time passed because they had made that internal discovery of possibility which no one could take away. That discovery would push them to go on to future tremendous seasons, but even more than that, their lives would never be the same. I have watched as some of these guys have gone on to become great athletes. However, more important, they all have succeeded as men who have become leaders in various areas of life. They embody all the things that I have found in others at the top. They have every quality found in all great teams that have won and leaders that have led.

I have a history with many great football teams and have spoken to several Southeastern Conference football champions and National Football League Super Bowl teams. However, the following group of players was none of those, but these players possessed the same qualities. These were the eighth and ninth grade basketball athletes who made up my first coaching job at Starkville High School in Mississippi. Over the first two years, we compiled an incredible record of wins. Opponents had a hard time beating us because we played not as individuals but as a group of young men who played as a team or family.

15

This group of former students honored me by presenting me with a plaque commemorating my years as their coach almost forty years later. Bill Buckley, a member of that wonderful team who now serves as state director for Fellowship of Christian Athletes in Mississippi, came to a banquet where I was speaking to present this plaque to me. He wrote these words that capture the essence of this chapter and this whole book.

The Toughest Coach I Ever Knew

> *Game after game, day after day, you did it his way, on his schedule, for his game plan. I can promise you one thing: I never thought of him and God in the same thought. His methods seemed heartless and his discipline unfair. He was undoubtedly the toughest coach I have ever known.*
>
> *But there was something that began to happen in us that season. Some unspoken, intangible force welled up inside us. It felt like the distant sound of a trumpet blast from deep down, calling us. It was a war sound, and somehow we knew that we were destined to answer it. It was bigger than us, transcending our simple high school days. It was a thing we longed for and feared at the same time—it was the unspoken part of Coach's game plan. We didn't know it then, but I believe now, that it was the call of God on our young hearts—a call to face Him and embrace our manhood.*
>
> *His demands on us became a thing of renown in our small hometown. He never cut us any slack, nor did he allow us to make excuses or blame others. He held us accountable every day in every way. I didn't like him very much at the time, this coach of ours. The cost of playing for him was great. He knew every weakness in our game, and he went after each one unmercifully and unrelentingly. He made war on anything that stood*

in the way of his team's ability to play to its potential.

A teammate's mom was five minutes late getting us to practice the morning after Thanksgiving one year. I remember sitting at his home aware that we were going to be late and thinking how unfair it was to be practicing during the holidays anyway. When she got us to the gym, the team was already running drills. We fell in, hoping that somehow Coach was too preoccupied to notice. Fat chance. After a two-hour practice and a full thirty minutes of conditioning, we were exhausted. Focusing my entire being on that door at the end of the gym, I pleaded with it to swallow me up and regurgitate me into the bowels of the locker room below. We were almost home free when we heard our names bounding off the walls and rafters like thunder off the mountains: "Buckley! Buchanan! On the line!" The memory of the pain and sweat of the next 30 minutes of "suicides" is as clear as if it happened an hour ago.

The cost of being a disciple of Jesus Christ is great. He knows every weakness in my life, and He attacks each one unmercifully and unrelentingly. He loves me too much to allow self-serving motives, diseased attitudes, and dangerous habits to live in my life. He makes war on anything that stands in the way of His great purposes for me. Hebrew 12:11 says, "All discipline for the moment seems not be joyful, but sorrowful; yet to those who have been trained by it, afterwards it yields the peaceful fruit of righteousness."

As I get more acquainted with my Savior Jesus Christ, I sure am thinking about Coach more and more and about how God used his tough love to confront selfishness, bad habits, and half-heartedness in me. This coach went on to become a pastor and then the chaplain for the football teams of Florida State University, South Carolina

17

University, and Mississippi State University. He is now a national evangelist and speaker. He is a Fellowship of Christian Athletes' national board member. You might know him as Ken Smith. I will always know him as Coach. He taught us the meaning of Colossians 3:23,"Whatever you do, do it with all of your heart for God, not men."

Thank you, Coach Smith, for never letting up on me and for pointing my teammates and me toward manhood and toward the Champion, Jesus Christ. I love you.

Chapter 2
Dream-Maker or Dream-Taker

"Those who love to talk will experience the consequences, for the tongue can kill or nourish life."
-Proverbs 18:21 (NLT)

"A leader is someone who has people following. If nobody is following then you are not a leader. A leader possesses a vision of what needs to be; has the gift to communicate the vision to those he leads and then has the ability to work with his followers to develop the best plan for accomplishing the vision. Vision and communication are a must for a leader; having all the answers on how to accomplish the vision is not a must. But the willingness to give ownership to the followers to the 'how' and allowing them to 'run' with it is the greatest way to fulfill the vision. Leaders possess integrity, core values, a 'can do' attitude, accountability and vision. They see what can be and go for it." -Jim Ramsey, Pastor, First Baptist Church, Thomson, Georgia

I have become very intrigued with Lewis and Clark, the explorers, who with great courage mapped the Louisiana Purchase by exploring this strange land. They led fascinating lives filled with courage. However, the driving force behind this great adventure was President Thomas Jefferson, the master of Monticello, who foresaw a large nation with one people governed by one set of laws. He was the **dream-maker** who with these words motivated Lewis and Clark:

> However our present interests may restrain us within our own limits, it is impossible not to look forward to distant times, when our rapid multiplication will expand itself beyond those limits and cover the whole northern, if not the southern, continent, with a people speaking the same

language, governed in similar forms and by similar laws.

Mind you, this was 1801 when two out of three Americans lived within fifty miles of the Atlantic Ocean. No roads existed across the Allegheny Mountains. No accurate map existed. Jefferson's great dream-making changed the lives of two men by inspiring them to create a map of unexplored territory, and they in turn changed a nation through their actions!

To become a leader, you too must fulfill the task of planting or making a dream. Through that task you shape lives. Every leader must plant dreams in order to create winners. You must also shape the dreams of the people you lead. You must impact those dreams.

My friend Steve Cloud, pastor of Northside Baptist Church in West Columbia, South Carolina, says that people must have a dream in order to have a passion about anything they do. Dream-making is about making sure that people have a passion for their dreams.

Dream-making is a daunting task. How do you do it? People at the top build winners through dream-making. In business, sports, or churches, these leaders have an ability to give people dreams. However, you must be careful. People who are good **dream-makers** are hard to find; but **dream-takers** are everywhere.

Billy Graham found property nestled in the mountains outside of Asheville, North Carolina and dreamed of building a conference center there that would train people in the faith through Bible study and worship. He instilled that dream within his staff, and today that dream has become a reality with the building of "The Cove."

Charles Roesel came to First Baptist Church in Leesburg, Florida, around twenty-five years ago and dreamed of a ministry-based evangelistic church. Today that congregation has a Ministry Village located on the church properties. This Ministry Village has been written about and taught about in Southern Baptist Seminaries for over a decade. Another great dream-maker, Steve Cloud dreams of building an entirely new church complex in the West Columbia area in the future.

Fisher DeBerry, Bobby Bowden, Chuck Amato, and Mark Richt, head coaches at various universities, have built dreams in the lives of the members of their teams every year. They have given their teams the dreams of being champions. However, even if the team cannot win its conference or have a winning record, the coach can give his players a dream. Tommy Bowden, coach at Clemson University, taught a dream in the middle of what seemed to be a disastrous season. With the planting of a dream, he led his team to wins over Florida State University, University of South Carolina, and Tennessee during the end of the 2003 season. He instilled the dream of winning even though the odds were against his team.

Dream-making is a difficult task, but, as you have seen, you can do it by using the correct skills. Even if you do not realize it, you are all dream-makers. Every great manager puts into the heart of his team members a dream, which they can use in all situations. A parent's dream-giving can give a child a chance of being very successful in life. Many high school coaches must give their team dreams so they can have a chance at greatness.

The way to give a dream to someone is fairly easy:
- Assess his or her talents, experience, and behavioral style.
- Define what you want him or her to accomplish.
- Be specific about the expected result and what you wish to accomplish with the task.

As grandparents my wife and I have made an amazing discovery. When we tell children **"no"** all the time and never reward good behavior, they get discouraged. So when our grandchildren do what is right, we applaud them as though they were giving a command performance. We are building a dream in them to do what is correct. Remember; give rewards as part of the dream-making.

Fellowship of Christian Athletes, Bobby Bowden, and others have made famous "Influence," a picture of a little boy who is wearing a much-too-large jersey and standing in the background watching several older students in a Fellowship of Christian Athletes huddle meeting. Coach Bowden tells his audiences that little eyes are on them. As the picture suggests, someone usually sees all actions. These actions cause reactions. Positive reactions often cause the observer to find a dream. Everyone has a part in teaching someone else a dream. Parents, teachers, bosses, coaches, scout leaders, big brothers, big sisters, and many others are all dream-makers. Use your actions to cause positive reactions in building dreams.

Sometimes even a casual remark may help someone realize a dream. For years, I have sent voice mail over phone systems to several companies. I call these messages an "encouraging word." Reponses often completely "blow me away." I am sometimes told that my words are the only positive words heard by some people all week. Often these same people tell me that my words have helped them to keep going.

You must spend time on **defining, modeling, identifying, and teaching** the dream. To define a dream, you must write it out. Include the people you are leading in the writing process. For a number of years at Carson Newman College in Jefferson City, Tennessee, Ken Sparks and his staff have selected senior football players and placed them as leaders over huddles, groups of twelve or thirteen guys. These leaders meet with Coach Sparks throughout the season to define the dreams for the team and to determine the rules. They then work with their huddles to accomplish the determined goals. He trains this group of seniors to lead by allowing them to help define the goals for the season and to help assess the progress toward reaching those goals.

A pastor called me to share his thoughts on the need to delay a building program until his congregation got their ministry in place. He was afraid if they did not get their priorities in place they would focus on the wrong things. His dream was definable, but he needed to get his message to the congregation. I suggested a town hall meeting, or even several meetings, in which he could share with them the best way that he perceived to accomplish their goal. He felt that each age group needed to see the value of changing the dream to fit the direction the church was headed. I simply advised him to define the dream, so they could claim it and then let them help. Involving everyone ensures that the dream can be accomplished.

You are a dream-maker, my friend, every day of your life. Whether you are the boss or student, neighbor or golfing buddy, you may be the catalyst that keeps the dream alive. You are helping build a dream.

The Bridge Builder

An old man, going a lone highway,
Came, at the evening, cold and gray,
To a chasm, vast, and deep, and wide,
Through which was flowing a sullen tide.

The old man crossed in the twilight dim;
The sullen stream had no fears for him;
But he turned, when safe on the other side,
And built a bridge to span the tide.

"Old man," said a fellow pilgrim, near,
"You are wasting strength with building here;
Your journey will end with the ending day;
You never again must pass this way;
You have crossed the chasm, deep and wide-
Why build you a bridge at the eventide?"

The builder lifted his old gray head:
"Good friend, in the path I have come," he said,
"There followeth after me today,
A youth, whose feet must pass this way.

This chasm, that has been naught to me,
To that fair-haired youth may a pitfall be.
He, too, must cross in the twilight dim;
Good friend, I am building the bridge for him."
Will Allen Dromgoole

Building bridges is a part of dream-making. A failure to grasp that you are part of the plan can kill a dream. If you do not build a bridge for others to cross over pitfalls, you may become a dream-taker instead of a dream-maker.

A winning tradition can be a **model** for others to follow to become champions. From my early days at Starkville High School in Mississippi, where the Yellowjackets consistently won, from the glory days with the teams of the late Nick Hyder in Valdosta, Georgia, from the mysticism of Saturday nights in Tallahassee with Florida State, and from the festive times with the Duke Blue Devils in Cameron Indoor Stadium, I have learned that the model of a winning team transfers into the lives of the athletes on that team. High standards with hard work model the way the leaders expect the athletes to respond. The responses of the athletes result in a unified team with a positive outlook.

The tragic breakdown of families today sometimes causes a lack of a family role model. Often no model exists either because of a divorce or because of parents with misplaced priorities. In situations where no models exist, you must model the accepted behavior for those you are leading so they can become winners.

What, then, are the tasks that every dream-maker ought to undertake? One task that you must accomplish is the defining of the goals and the making of them attainable. You must be able to assess the situation and to help your team, employee, or even a child see the direction he or she desires to go. You, as the dream-maker, must point them in the right direction and encourage them to go in that direction.

My son Richard was a skinny kid when he was young. He grew up watching the Florida State Seminoles where I was chaplain. He decided early on that he wanted to play college football as a wide receiver. However, skinny, slow kids are not prime candidates to play that position. He learned basic techniques when he played on a state championship team as a sophomore in high school in Tallahassee, Florida, but then we moved to Gainesville, Florida, to a high school that did not throw the ball very much. Richard really wanted to play college ball. To encourage him and to give his spirits a lift, I gave him a shirt that he wore under his shoulder pads for four years. Its message on the front simply stated "Playing for a Chance." This defined his goal. He followed through on his dream and got his chance to play for one of the finest programs in the country, Carson Newman College.

You must be able to help people define their dreams and work toward reaching those dreams. That is the true purpose of a dream-maker.

As a dream-maker you must never forget that you are the teacher. You must never get out of the role of **teacher – student, mentor – pupil.** You must constantly **learn, teach, establish relationships, appraise,** and **model behavior.**

Another task of the dream-maker is the gathering of information and the giving of that information to others. Read books, articles, and websites that will help the people that you lead. **Learn** and then **teach** others. You must do these things to be a good leader. Explain the expected behavior in simple language so that the followers can easily understand. They can then use the things that you have gathered and have taught them to reach the expected goal.

A third task would be to spell out or **establish the relationship** between you and your team, congregation, or employees. As a leader explain exactly what you expect from them. A district manager asked me how he should conduct his first meeting with his sales force. I suggested that he start with the truth. I even suggested that he begin with this statement: "Please understand this is the way I see it. If I do not help you succeed, I will not succeed; so when I tell you to do something or suggest a behavior, please remember this and put it at the top of the list as to why I said do it! This may sound silly or redundant, but my job is based upon it. I will teach you what will help us succeed. I may make a mistake, but your success will be my driving force!"

As parents, you would do well to make sure that you know your responsibility in your children's lives as well. Your children should understand exactly what is expected of them.

Do not forget that as a leader another task would be to **appraise** constantly the progress of the people you are leading. Make them aware that you are appraising. Keep good records of meetings with them. Give them evaluations based on the goals you have given them.

When I first started working with Florida State University in the early 1980s, I spelled out my role as chaplain in my first meeting with the team:

Our (the school's and my) purpose is not just to give you an opportunity to be a part of an outstanding football program; our purpose is to make you contribute to the greatest nation in the world. We want you to finish college and, above all else, be the finest man you can be--academically, morally, and personally. We want you to be a total person. Yes, the goals we set should become the base for a solid foundation. We will evaluate you on how well you do on this basis.

Assessment is extremely hard to accomplish. Without a planned strategy, assessment will not happen. I know that some companies have a built-in evaluation process which should certainly be followed. However, the relationship aspect is also a part of that evaluation. It may not be planned, but those who succeed in winning and leading are those who constantly reassess their own behavior and those of the candidates under their tutelage.

A parent, a coach, a team member, or a friend must **evaluate** on a fairly regular basis or find himself or herself in a rut. We all know that a rut is a grave with both ends kicked out! If you as the leader do not assess progress, behavior, and growth, you will have set a dangerous precedent.

A final task is a summary of a leader's behavior. A leader who produces a winner literally **models** that idea every moment of the day. You, as a leader, must teach all of the concepts by the way you live.

Bobby Bowden's actions and words at Florida State University have always impressed me. During every part of his day, whether he is dealing with the press, talking with a coach, or working with the team; what you see is what you get. He is what he is. He never puts on "airs," as we say in the South. If you meet him on a plane, in his office, or at the ball field during competition, he is always the same.

A young coach described his visit with Mark Richt, head coach at the University of Georgia. Because of the upcoming game with Auburn, the Bulldogs seemed a little tense. The young coach said that he was uptight for the team because it was a game that would determine Georgia's participation in the Southeastern Conference Championship game. Coach Richt approached the

26

young coach as he stood on the sidelines watching practice. Instead of focusing on the practice and his players, Coach Richt talked calmly about the rising moon in the late evening. He commented, "God's handiwork is amazing isn't it?" The young coach found him surprisingly calm and unperturbed by a somewhat tense situation. Mark was modeling his leadership. No coach that I know shows more confidence or serenity than he does because he has done his work. He knows what his team has to do to win in any given situation; however, his main focus in life is his faith. It is part of who he is. He does exactly what he has been taught. That consistency goes a long way in setting tones for his team.

Ken Sparks, head coach at Carson Newman, certainly is another person who models his faith. I have watched Ken in many different situations. I have seen him talking with a group of coaches, working with athletes at a Fellowship of Christian Athlete camp, or confronting hard issues with a dissident player. What you see is what you get. He models what he teaches.

For over eighteen years, I have conducted various events with the Billy Graham association and their area crusades. I have worked with youth coordinators and crusade directors and have ridden in the van from the airport with office crews, secretaries, and research people. The thing that impresses me most about their style is that they practice what they teach. Yes, modeling is essential in creating a winner.

Certainly if you want to be a successful parent, you must model what you teach. I think my wife and I have done a fair job as parents. My wife Donnelle and I have been married over forty years, and, my friend, I have seen and learned well what it means to model the way you want your children to live. This lady has a remarkable unwavering consistency about her. She has done some fabulous teaching. This lady is remarkable when it comes to teaching by modeling. She exhibits patience even in the toughest situations. If you wish to teach your children kindness, she is a good example. She is always respectful and tender toward everyone she meets. This lady models all the things that I am writing about. Her actions are the epitome of truthfulness, courteousness, responsibility, and character from sunup to sundown. She lives what she wants our children to learn. I love the way my children are maturing. I like who they are as people.

I spoke to a group of coaches when the concept of fighting drugs within the schools was just beginning.

I will never forget the shocked looks on the faces of coaches when I said, "Don't expect your kids to listen to you tell them not to be involved with drugs in any way if you use tobacco and drink beer. Your talking is shadowed by your modeling."

As a leader you are a mentor. You teach, but you are also a monitor. You have to teach by what you do and then monitor your learners to see if they are getting what you are teaching!

You as a leader not only participate in selling the dream, but you also participate in the task of putting the dream into the lives of the people you are called to influence.

Once your goal is established, hardships and life-changing hard work, and even difficult tasks become second place. The dream becomes all-important. This is an important lesson I learned hanging around people who are at the top!

Yes, dream-making should be your focus, but don't become a dream-taker! Dr. Martin Luther King stood on some steps in Washington D.C. and proclaimed a dream which transformed our culture and our lives. What if earlier someone had discouraged him from trying to change the plight of African-Americans by telling him that he would be wasting his time? A dream to break the barrier of the four-minute mile propelled Jim Ryan into the record books. What if earlier a coach had discouraged him by criticizing his running ability? Be careful that you don't give negative feedback.

The failure to define the dream that you want to accomplish may rob someone of the ability to dream. I mentioned that in dealing with dream-making, you have to define the dream. I want to give a little more time to that idea. I once heard a coach ask his team, "Don't you want to win the State Championship?" The kids all shouted, "Yes!" He was attempting to give his athletes a dream, but he didn't take this point any further. Far too often the dream-maker does not define the worthy goal or explain how to obtain that goal. That coach should have given his team the ways and means to reach that important goal. He did not define or explain how to obtain the goal. His words were not a true giving of a dream.

Another example is the boss who tells the work force that they are going to be the best without spelling out what "being the best" means or how to reach those specified goals. He or she has made a major mistake in the building of dreams.

The parent who wants his or her child to be a good student without defining exactly what a good student means also makes a major mistake. You must explain exactly what must be done to obtain a dream.

Often people have a dream but no one to help them find ways to make the dream a reality. Bear in mind that I am a product of the era when plays such as *Camelot* and *Man of La Mancha* were popular. I grew up on the hope of a better time tomorrow. One line from *Camelot,* "The rain may never fall until after sundown," drove our thoughts and dreams. Nothing would "rain on our parades." Almost everyone had a dream in those days, even if it were impossible, but today, I encounter people all the time who either have never had a dream or who have lost their dreams. They have not reached the place that they had hoped to reach. I remember listening to a country and western song about an entire class of seniors who had dreams when they graduated, but then most of them settled for far less than they had anticipated. The song spells the tragedy of life. People lost their dreams for a number of reasons, but they lost their dreams nevertheless. It is always a tragedy to meet someone who has lost a dream.

Have you ever observed a young child playing a game on an outdoor basketball court or a tennis court? While he/she is involved in the game, that youngster thinks he/she is Michael Jordon or Serena Williams. If an older child comes by and tells the younger child that he/she is too short, or not strong enough to ever be any good, that youngster starts to lose the dream. The dream-taker has caused the child to question himself or herself. If that happens, a dream-giver can enter that child's life and give back the dream by encouraging and working with him or her until finally the child can visualize the dream again. You must be that dream-giver, not the dream-taker. Remind the people whom you are leading to follow Don Quixote's advice, dream the impossible dream!

Perhaps the saddest thing one can encounter is a person with a lost dream. Unfortunately I, meeting people in business, in churches, and even in athletics, have seen people who have lost their dreams. They can be compared to balloons with the air let out. They simply no longer have synergy or energy. They have lost the edge that all must have to lead or win. Don't allow anyone to take away your dreams, and don't you become a dream-taker.

One of my fondest memories is my encounter with Sam Rixie. I coached him at Leesburg High School in Florida during the 1960s. My encounter with Sam was my personal lesson in dream-taking or possibly in dream-making. I was a young high school coach enthusiastic about my defense, which required one player, known as a monster man, to be set free to make most of the tackles. With slants and movement in the line, he should make a large number of tackles. I explained to the team in that first meeting that this kid would have to be the meanest, toughest kid on the team. When the meeting broke up and the kids went to get dressed, this small kid stayed behind. I thought Sam might want the position of water boy. Instead, he told me that he wanted to be my monster man on the defense. I couldn't believe that he even wanted to try this because of his size. I explained how I was sorry, but he was just too small. Time proved how wrong I was and how great he would become. But I almost took away his dream.

It seems strange to me to observe people who want to be successful leaders, but who are dream-takers. What about the district manager who decides that the personality differences he/she has with a new sales person causes him/her more problems than he/she wants to deal with, and, as a result, he/she robs that person of his/her dream? What about the pastor who "beats his congregation up" with words explaining how badly they behave and how unwillingly they do the Lord's work? What about the teacher who tells a group of students that they cannot do the work because of their lack of effort? And what about the parents who should lead their kids to new places but belittle them and talk about things that they cannot do and how badly they behave. Some suggest these actions produce "a self-fulfilling prophecy." People become what you expect. That is tragic to say the least! If you don't believe in someone, you can cause that person to give up.

Some people make **mistakes in the dream-making process.** They rob dreams from the folks whom they wish to make into winners and leaders. Sometimes people fail to understand that

30

they are dream-makers. Often people in leadership positions stun me by their failure to realize that people watch them for dreams.

When it comes to teenagers, our culture doesn't promote a dreamer. In fact, it could be argued that we are a culture that appeals to the median kid. Creativity often gets negative feedback and dreams are discouraged. Adults become dream-takers instead of dream-makers, but whenever you take the time, you will notice that having dreams can make better students and happier people. Without a dream a person just gets by in life. This lack of dreams often causes lethargy, which means nothing gets accomplished. You should be in the business of giving dreams to teenagers, not discouraging them.

A failure to define the dream will cause the people you wish to help to fail. You will become the dream-taker if you fail to understand that you must deal with people who need to understand where you are going. Whatever else is going on, it is not about the great tomorrow and what is happening out there. It is about today and getting people to accomplish a purpose. That means that you have to see and care for people and to recognize them as individuals.

Have you heard the story of the family who went to a fancy restaurant? The adults were so busy enjoying the ambience that they failed to notice how uncomfortable their ten-year-old son was with his situation. They spent their time observing the extensive menu instead of their child. In the meantime, he spent his time looking around at other people's food trying to figure out what he could possibly eat. When the waiter arrived, the adults placed orders for Steak Diane, accompanied by a fancy salad, for everyone, including the son. As the mother was ordering for the child, the waiter knelt down eye-to-eye with the child and asked him if he knew what he really wanted.

The child shyly answered, "Well, I really want a hamburger and French fries."

The parents were stunned and embarrassed because of such a mundane order in this fancy restaurant.

Then to make matters worse, the waiter asked if the boy would also like a chocolate shake?

"Wow," answered the child, "I sure would!"

31

"Coming right up!" answered the waiter, who then walked away.

Before the parents could begin to scold, the child spoke these wise words, "I like him. He thinks I am a real person!"

Those whom I have observed at the top are people who sell dreams to real people. They never forget with whom they are working. They pay close attention to what happens, and they listen to their hearts as well as their minds. They never fail to care before they start teaching what they know.

Chapter 3
Revving Your Engine in a Stalled World!

"Like a bad tooth or a lame foot is reliance on the unfaithful in times of trouble." -Proverbs 25:19 (NIV)

"Real leaders are folks who can take the 'bad' and make it good and take the 'good' and make it better. They are characterized by a great faith that depends on a great God that makes everything a possibility—even when circumstances and emotions scream otherwise." -Ken Sparks, Head Football Coach, Carson Newman College

Our world is stalled. Yes, if you plan to make winners, you must accept a reality: Our world is stalled. About the time it looks as though we will find a way to get things worked out, a war begins or a disease arrives on the scene to threaten our lives. A Middle East conflict always seems to be brewing. Oil shortage, either real or engineered, and the resulting economic struggles affect everyone. The attack on the World Trade Center, September 11, 2001, and other imminent threats of unknown terrorists have caused the world to put things on hold. Every time the newscasters talk of the possibility of a threat, everyone has to go through the thought pattern of whether to drive or to fly on that next trip. Often people decide to wait until things calm down. We have allowed terrorists to stall our lives.

Many of you reading this book have dealt with the change in the economy, which has forced you to go out in search of employment. One of my friends holds a graduate degree in computer science, but he has to search for contract jobs to survive. His assessment of the situation intrigues me. He tells me that he has put everything on hold until the world changes.

A catastrophic disease or a death can also stall your life. The unexpected loss of a parent, spouse, or child will cause people to put things on hold. When things of this nature occur, I always talk about life's report card, which we all get at one point or another, the report card with the terrible "D's" on it:

- Divorce
- Death
- Disease
- Disillusionment
- Disappointment

Or the one with those awful "F's":

- Fear
- Failure
- Frustration
- Fatigue

All of these things can cause your life to stall. When you stall, you lose the power to teach, to sell dreams, and to lead. You produce no winners; therefore, you must get your life on track before you can lead.

My mission statement has **encouragement** at its core. My purpose in life is to encourage people in their faith and life. I really believe that one of the things that I am supposed to do in life is to be an encouragement to people. How in the world do I do that with people who are stalled? I want to meet you in that stalled world to help you figure out how to "rev up your engine."

One of my favorite football stories is the one about the three players who were taking a class in sociology. The professor decided to give the guys a break by testing orally.

Each was to answer one question from a sociological position. The question was the same for all three. "Suppose your body were lying in a casket. People are passing by the casket and looking at your body. What would you wish for them to say from a sociological position?"

The first player quickly responded, "I want them to remember that the family is the most important part of a society. Therefore, I want them to say I was a wonderful family man." The professor was greatly impressed and promptly gave that student an A.

The second player responded quickly as well, "I know the extreme importance of the economy to any society. I, therefore, hope they will look at my casket and say that I was a fair and honest businessman." That earned this student an A as well.

The third player did not quickly answer, but when prompted by the professor, his reply was the best of all, "When they pass by my casket, I want them to say, 'I think that sucker is moving!'"

Life–that is what I want in my life.

When the world is in a rut, I want people to say, "That sucker is moving! He shows signs of life."

I really want that for me and for you as well.

Leaders who produce winners figure out how to keep their lives moving and advancing toward their visions and goals. In business, a manager expects his employees to reach certain goals in sales. A coach wants to implant information and the desire to reach certain goals and objectives in the minds and hearts of the members of his team. The pastor wants his church moving toward implementation of whatever the members have determined as the mission statement of the church. How can you do all of that?

In a stalled word I am convinced of the need for a **base on which to build.** I am totally amazed that people try to lead and produce winners without a conscious decision of who they are and what matters to them. In order to lead, you must have a solid base.

The Bible says that a man who is wise builds his house on a rock. The failure to build on that the rock is a lack of faith. Let me put it plainly and simply. The people whom I have met at the top have a faith that is a fundamental part of their lives.

In 1982, head football coach Bobby Bowden at Florida State University gave me an opportunity that would change the direction of my life. Coach Bowden gave me the position as chaplain for the football team. I served as the team's chaplain for five years. While there, every member of his staff influenced my life. I watched as Coach Bowden built an exciting football program. Under Coach Bowden's leadership each of his assistant coaches made his own special contribution: Coach Jim Gladden was a master at building relationships with young people. Coach Mickey Andrews was a stern demanding taskmaster. Coach John Eason was a skilled receivers' teacher. Coach Chuck Amato was a great defensive coach. Coach Billy Sexton was a consistent loyal performer. Coach Brad Scott was a great recruiter. Coach Mark Richt was a learner and implementer of dreams who was destined for greatness. As a result of that experience I also met Tommy

Bowden and countless other graduate assistants who have gone on to lead successful lives.

I saw a team develop. I saw All-Americans such as Deion Sanders, Sammy Smith, Greg Allen, and Paul McGowan. These players were great then, but they became even better players because of the coaching they received. It was a great and exciting time for me and for that program. Without a doubt, the base of the entire operation then and now is Coach Bowden's faith. He is unapologetic about the need for a chaplain to be a part of the football program. He believes teaching the Christian faith is essential. These meetings are not coerced or demanded, just available. His faith is a part of his dealing with kids and their diversity. Coach Bowden makes decisions based on his faith and demands the same from his coaches. I was there when Billy Graham, the great evangelist, and other outstanding men of faith such as Clebe McClary, a decorated war veteran, Grant Teaff, director of the College Football Association, and countless others shared their faith. That base is important to the development of the program. Clint Purvis, the current chaplain, and other leaders of the Fellowship of Christian Athletes have had a huge impact on that program as well.

Coach Bowden is not the only coach who runs his athletic program based on Christian principles. Jim Tressel at Ohio State University, Tommy Bowden at Clemson University, Fisher DeBerry at Air Force Academy, and Ken Sparks at Carson Newman College, just to mention a few, have seen this base as an essential element in their athletic programs.

I have been doing this thing called life for over sixty years. I have been a minister for over thirty years. I have watched people build their lives on everything but what really matters. I have conducted funerals for a long time, but I have never seen a hearse pulling a U-Haul trailer. You are not going to take anything with you when you die, so you need to make sure that you have built your life on what matters. In all my years as I have stood by folks who were dying, I have never heard anyone say that they wish they had spent more time hustling in life. However, there have been many who have said that they wish they had spent more time on things that mattered: family, faith, and friends. When it is all over, you need to have built your life on things that really matter.

War, attacks, terrorists – those things that we fear will not be resolved with duck tape or plywood covers for windows, but they will be resolved with faith that is alive and well.

Have you heard about the farmer who was looking for a new hired hand? He posted a notice for help in the local barbershop. Only one person applied.

The farmer asked, "Do you have any experience?"

The man replied, "I do not, but I sleep when the wind blows."

The farmer had no idea what he meant, but he needed help so he hired the man.

Six months later during a storm, loud thunder and lightening awakened the farmer. He immediately got up and went to check on the hay. It was securely covered with a tarp. He then checked on the livestock. They were safely in the barn.

Stopping by the bunkhouse, he awakened the new hand and asked, "Did you put the tarp over the hay and put the livestock in the barn?"

Smiling, the young man answered, "Yes, I did. Remember, I told you that I sleep when the wind blows."

When the storms come and the wind blows, your life will fail unless you have a moral center and base for your life. If you want to get your life together, build on a solid base. God should be placed before anything in your life. If you do this, all other things will fall into place.

In the Bible, Job says, "For the life of every living thing is in His hand, and the breath of all humanity." -Job 12:10 (NLT)

Later, Jeremiah says:

> [7]*But blessed are those who trust in the LORD and have made the LORD their hope and confidence.* [8]*They are like trees planted along a riverbank, with roots that reach deep into the water. Such trees are not bothered by the heat or worried by long months of drought. Their leaves stay green, and they go right on producing delicious fruit.*
> -Jeremiah 17: 7-8 (NLT)

You will "rev up your engine" when you build upon a base. To get your engine running in a stalled world, you have to devise a strategy or a battle plan. Far too many people live their lives with no offense. They just play defense and, therefore, never get above their circumstances. They just allow the circumstances to control them. Do you take the time to write out what your direction, organization, or time allotment is going to be? Most people have an idea of what they are doing, but they seldom write it down or reform it.

Bob Biehl's *Masterplanning (The Complete Guide for Building a Strategic Plan for Your Business, Church, or Organization)* has an acrostic for living that he recommends:

DOCTOR

D = Direction	*What should we do next?* *Why?*
O = Organization	*Who is responsible for what?* *Who is responsible for whom?* *Do we have the right people in the right places?*
C = Cash	*What is our projected income, expense, net?* *Can we afford it?* *How can we afford it?*
T = Tracking	*Are we on target?*
O = Overall Evaluation	*Are we achieving the quality we expect and demand of ourselves?*
R = Refinement	*How can we be more effective and more efficient (move toward the ideal)?*

I am amazed at how many people I meet who do not have a plan for anything, not their lives, their jobs, their marriages, their parenting, not anything. Do you know what to expect from your teenagers when you have toddlers? Don't wait until the problem arises before you make a plan. You need a base and a battle plan now!

You will "rev up your engine" of life if you learn how to behave. Now that sounds so silly, but I am amazed at the people I meet whose behavior is deplorable toward cab drivers, waitresses, or clerks in stores; but, even worse, towards their families, friends, and people with whom they work. Every strategy has a center. At your center you need to teach that people, regardless of status, must be treated with respect and a genuine feeling of concern. If you do this, you will create an environment that will forge bonds.

- People on your team need to know that they matter!
- People in your organization need to know that they matter!
- People in your church need to know that they matter!
- People in your house need to know that they matter!

Be courteous. Even my grandchildren know the magic words: "please," "thank you," "I'm sorry," and "you matter."

Once upon a time a professor of medicine was teaching the introductory anatomy class for medical students. It was a "real bear" to pass. When it came time for the exam, all the students had prepared well. When they arrived, they were stunned to learn that the opening question was a simple one. What is the name of the lady who cleans up the study area everyday? When an enraged student protested the absurdity of the question, the professor answered that to know anatomy without knowing real people was irrelevant.

The point is clear. Behavior is very important. Proper behavior toward people is necessary to lead them. Treating them fairly and with respect goes a long way.

Have balance. For far too many years leaders have not talked about balance enough. Balance consists of spending time planning ways to give time to what is needed. For example, after September 11, 2001, people in New York City slowed down and paid attention to some things that they had neglected, such as family, friends, nature, and religion. However, much too soon people were back to the same old "rat race." The slowing down to "smell the roses" ended. People should have learned a lesson from that event. It's true that you will not succeed in any business unless you work at it. However, don't do this at the expense of losing your focus on important things: families, spouses, children, friends, and religion. *health*

As I look back over my life, I wish that I could do some things differently. In certain aspects, my life has been successful. My coaching record in football and basketball has far more wins than losses. Churches that I have pastored have all doubled in size. But because I let the balance falter in my life, I could have lost my family. I let squeaky wheels get the attention instead of the folks who mattered. My life became filled with unhappy people who complained that I was neglecting them. This caused my life to be unhappy too. I was miserable and not doing anything very well. My life improved greatly once I put things more in balance. My friend Steve Brown says we all are a bunch of turkeys, and we just have to learn to live with it.

There was once a fellow in Mississippi who became involved with a turkey hunt. It seems that the sun was setting as a farmer was admiring his just-finished plowed field when a shotgun blast broke the silence. Right before his eyes, a turkey fluttered to its death in the middle of his field. Out of the woods and onto the field walked a well-dressed lawyer.

The farmer exclaimed, "Don't you dare walk on my field. That is now my turkey!"

The lawyer exclaimed, "I am from the law firm of Debusy, Debusy and Debusy. I am here on a turkey hunt. I shot that turkey; therefore, it is mine!"

"You better not walk on the field which belongs to me!" exclaimed the farmer. The argument continued, raging back and forth.

The lawyer yelled, "I will sue you if you don't give me that turkey!"

"We do not sue here. Instead we will have a kicking contest. We each get a kick until the other gives up," answered the farmer.

Thinking he could do that and easily beat the old farmer, the lawyer yelled back, "That's great! You go first!"

The farmer reared back and kicked the lawyer right in the gut. When the lawyer bent over, the farmer quickly kicked him in the mouth!

Bleeding and staggering, the lawyer grunted, "It's my turn now!"

"Shoot!" exclaimed the farmer. "It doesn't matter anymore. You can have the turkey!"

Reality means that the world will make all kind of demands of you and will probably contribute to keeping your life out of balance. Let them keep the turkey, and make sure that you claim what is important. One of the things you might do is make a list of the things in your life that you feel are important. Take a look at the schedule you keep and make sure that you have a balance in what you are doing. Some turkeys just aren't worth kicking!

Family

Health

Relationships & hearing God

Order in home, finances, exercise

Rest, recreation

Looking forward to events

Writing Goals

Having enough resources to do what God inspires.

Helping family, friends, needy

Chapter 4
Have a Plan, Plan the Plan, Work the Plan, But It Is Still the People!

"The generous prosper and are satisfied; those who refresh others will themselves be refreshed."
- Proverb: 11:25 (NLT)

"A great leader is a man who is willing to stand true to his beliefs, convictions, and values, regardless of the circumstances. A great leader is also a person that cares and motivates others with great enthusiasm and love for life, making them do things they sometimes didn't think they could achieve." -Fisher DeBerry, Head Football Coach, Air Force Academy

Always whenever I start thinking of people skills and the leaders I have met who exhibit them, I think of Fisher DeBerry and his staff at the Air Force Academy. These coaches through their people skills are masters at developing each player's talent way beyond expectations so the player becomes a tough competitor.

A couple of years ago I took my brother Mac with me on my annual visit to speak to the Air Force Academy football team. During that special weekend, the Academy had a big game on Saturday. They needed to beat Utah State for conference recognition. The game was being televised on the East Coast, which entailed early playing of the game. I remember thinking that I was sorry that we would have little chance to be with Coach DeBerry and his staff because of their busy schedule. However, I will never forget that in the middle of the hustle and bustle of that big television game, they treated my brother and me as special guests. Coach DeBerry took time to be with us, to talk with us, and to treat us with respect.

My brother said, "Man, I bet playing for this guy would be special. I wish I could have played for him."

It is true. Coach DeBerry makes people feel special and invests in their lives with his time and shows his concern about their lives. His players delight in playing for him.

The single most important characteristic shared by leaders at the top of winning organizations is strong **caring** about their people. Bobby Bowden, coach at Florida State University, calls everybody "Bud," but his concern for people is always evident. One recruiting Saturday when all the top prospects were visiting Florida State University, Coach Bowden and I were going to be in Quincy, Florida, for a fish fry to raise money for a little girl who was sick. Someone had scheduled two important events on the same day! I did my best to hustle Coach Bowden out of the building to get back to those great recruits. He, on the other hand, took the time to meet and sign autographs as if it were the only thing he had to do that day. The day was all about rushing for me, but not for Coach Bowden. People are important to him, and he spends time making them feel important. He coaches that way. He makes each player feel that they are at the heart of the team, not on the periphery. Everyone feels that he or she makes a difference to the success of the organization. When that happens, people feel centered and that gives their work meaning.

One very successful businessman periodically lets me go to his conventions. His income in one year is greater than mine over the last several, but if you want to find him at his conventions, don't look in the VIP booth. Look for him in the check-in lines at the hotel, in the coffee shop, or in the hallways talking with the people who work in his organization. He has found the key to success: Care about your people! Spend time relating to them. When I am there, I see him at the registration desk or in the dining area, wherever people are. What is he always doing? He is talking to people. He cares about them!

You must create a partnership between people and their dreams. People far too often do not realize what makes other people "tick." The company officials often do not evaluate the strengths and weaknesses of the company and the people who work there. To be a successful leader, you must understand people and help them become focused in order for them to be fulfilled!

To build a great company, team, or church, you must start with who the individuals are and how they function. You must **build relationships** with everyone in the company, on the team, or in the church.

I want to see if I can help you understand a very important truth. Building relationships takes time and effort. You must decide to put forth this effort if you wish to succeed. This concept may not be stated on the agenda or the plan of action, but it makes the agenda work. In order to prove my point, I want to site two events:

- The team had lost three games by a close score-- field goals by the other teams in the last minute, a fumble on the goal line, really small issues, but losses nevertheless. The staff was trying to decide what to do when I suggested having a picnic! This is Division One football! This team is in serious trouble! I will never forget the looks on the faces of the coaches around the table when I suggested the picnic. My plan hinged on having practice start and then having a barbecue caterer drive out onto the practice field. I suggested having a roving DJ drive up as well. My purpose, easing the strain on the players, hinged on their having a good time just laughing and talking. After spending several minutes in debate, the coaches made the decision to follow my plan. I envisioned that the players and coaches would sit around, laughing and enjoying each other. Maybe they could even begin to learn and understand one another better. We had reached that decision early in the morning; however, when I got to practice, was I surprised! What had started out to be a picnic on the field had been changed to dinner in the indoor practice facility. The players ate by themselves; the coaches went up to their meeting rooms and waited for this horrible practice interruption to be over so they could coach these kids for the next game. I won't tell you much else except to say that that group of players did not win again and certainly never became a team.
- Another team, with which I also have had a long association, has every two-a-day practice session finish with time spent swimming in the student center swimming pool. The players and the coaches

45

spend time together laughing and enjoying each other. This allows them to learn one another and become a team. True, this takes time away from allotted practice time, but the team wins often. It is a team every year to be reckoned with, a force that is hard to beat.

Now listen, all you coaches who just had a heart attack that I have dared to suggest that you have more picnics and less practice, just be aware of my contention that building relationships makes practices easier and builds a force that holds the players together in the long run.

The lack of **building relationships** is not a problem peculiar to athletic teams. Building a team in business is just as important. I know of a major company that recently awarded its outstanding employees with a vacation at an outstanding resort. These were the company's top producers. However, the CEO failed to attend the function, and no interaction occurred between the sales people and upper management. This was a failed chance to produce loyalty and team pride at a very high cost to the company.

I visit many churches each year and I have made an amazing though not startling discovery. The pastor and staff that take the time to relate to their people are the places that the church is alive and vibrant. Glen Money at Monroe, Georgia, and Jim Ramsey at Thomson, Georgia, are two pastors that come to mind. These two gifted leaders spend a great amount of time being where their people are. They are active in civic clubs, attend ball games, and eat breakfast at local cafes often enough that waitresses know what they are going to order before they place the order. Their efforts have forged close relationships with the people in the community and helped make their churches stronger.

I was once asked what I would do before becoming the pastor of a church. I told them that I would first go to the cafe where many of the locals meet often for coffee and "catching up" on what is going on in the community. Understanding the people in the church is as important as understanding the doctrine of the church.

Church membership produces opportunities, but often churches have large congregations with no life. If I had my life to

46

do all over again, I would leave my office door open more as a pastor. I would become a pastor who invited people to interrupt. I may have preached good sermons, but I regret not building stronger relationships. To build those relationships, I suggest you:

- Learn names or at least have nametags worn by team members, company employees, or church members.
- Allotted time to develop relationships around mealtime is as important as dispensing information.
- Have team projects that help people gain understanding of how their teammates or co-workers function. One manager had each member of his team fill out a questionnaire about personal likes and dislikes as well as a list of the people he or she most admires.
- Read and discuss a book together. Athletes, staffs, and church members can do that. Casual conversation where you can learn how your followers interpret the books is not a waste of time.
- Plan to get to know your people. With a plan, annual picnics ought not be a waste of time.

To become a world-class leader, you must **understand your own motivations** and the motivations of your players, congregation, or employees. You can get what you want in life by helping others get what they want! You can do that if you understand how you function, understand your behavioral style, and figure out how these mesh or conflict with others. In kindergarten, my grandson learned that old adage: "Do unto others as you would have them do unto you." The way you do that is to properly relate to others through understanding of their behavior or what makes them "tick."

For years as I have worked with teams, churches and businesses, I have used a particular behavioral analysis profile model and found it to be a great tool for identifying and giving proper attention to the behavior styles of others, but many different behavior profiles are available. Choose the profile that best meets

47

your needs and incorporate it into your life and the lives of those you lead.

The idea that people are different is not new. Early writers talked of different ways of identifying personalities. The early Greeks believed that the human body was composed of four basic elements: air, water, fire, and earth. Hippocrates first set these theories down in a systematic way. He also believed that the body was composed of four corresponding components: blood, phlegm, yellow bile, and black bile, which controlled a person's mood and approach to life. These theories were the first systematic way of describing people and remained in use until the Middle Ages. Many different theories have existed since then, but the importance of learning about different personality types hasn't diminished.

To be a good leader, you must learn that everyone does not react the same way to the same situation. Each of us has a different behavioral style. I have one; my wife has a different one; my children have different ones from either of us; my prayer partner has another style, and on and on. I do not suggest that understanding behavior styles is easy to do, but you must realize that each person will react differently to the same stimulus. Therefore, in leading, coaching, teaching and relating, you need to find out with whom you are dealing and how that person will respond to your situation.

When I meet people, I do realize that they are not all extroverted goal-setters as I am. Some people are introverted and compliant. Some want to know details while others don't. I just try to be as sensitive as I can be and make them feel as comfortable as possible with the situation. If I want to motivate, change, teach, or lead them; I need to know which approaches to use to communicate with them. You, too, must learn to function in this manner.

You must try to understand what people believe and learn the motivations for their actions since these are essential components of the plans, which leaders use to create winners.

Building relationships with the people you lead and with your associates can be a daunting task, but a necessary one.

A difficult task I undertook involved building relationships among players at Mississippi State University. My friend Jackie Sherrill, then the coach at MSU, asked me to come to MSU under

48

contract to work as the director of player development. Both the program and the team were struggling. I tried to build relationships among the players and coaches.

I used something from a past experience as the backbone of my plan. Coach Dan Redding at Carson Newman College used personal contact to build relationships with his players. He coached my son Richard. Richard was not easy to deal with at that time. He was struggling with several personal issues, which I think would have caused him to crash and burn, if not for Dan and his personal relationship building. Dan ate with him, invited him into his home, came by his locker to talk, and tried to understand the difficulties that Richard was facing. He attempted to relate to him. Dan continued seeking out Richard in spite of Richard's sometimes lack of responsiveness. Dan's relationship with Richard enabled Richard to succeed.

Using Dan's example, I asked Coach Sherrill for a locker in the dressing room with the players. It takes a lot of "guts" for a fifty-five-plus-year-old, out-of-shape male to dress and shower in a room full of well-conditioned athletes, but I did it because I knew it would help build relationships. I also invited the athletes into my home and visited them in their dorm rooms. I ate with them at least once a week. I learned their names and often stopped by to talk with them during warm-ups.

I noticed another coach who used the same methods. Jim Tompkins, an assistant coach, was brilliant at building relationships with his segment of the squad. He used some of the same methods. His wife even baked cookies every Thursday for his group of players. According to my observation, Jim's players performed consistently on a squad that overall did not do well.

Encouraging people, especially difficult people, is hard work. It takes time and intensive effort, but I saw it work over and over again during that year. Justin Griffith, a player on that squad, has become a successful NFL player. I would like to think that my listening and encouraging words made some difference in his life.

Once a man fell into a pit and couldn't get himself out.

A Christian Scientist came along and said, "You only think that you are in a pit."

A Pharisee came by and said; "Only bad people fall into pits."

Next a Fundamentalist said, "You deserve your pit."

Later a Charismatic said, "Just confess that you're not in a pit."

A Methodist came by and said, "We brought you some food and clothing while you're in the pit."

A Presbyterian said, "This was no accident, you know."

An Optimist told him, "Things could be worse."

A Pessimist said, "Things will get worse!"

Jesus, seeing the man, took him by the hand and lifted him out of the pit.

You must be there to help those you lead whenever they need your help. To help lead and build winners:

- Learn what type personalities your followers have by using some behavior implement. Always think about the person with whom you are dealing.
  1. Are they a talker or listener?
  2. Do they set goals or do they respond?
  3. What matters to them?
  4. What experiences have they had in life?
- Devote time to building relationships.
  1. Coaches set a practice schedule that allows downtime.
  2. Sales meetings should include some time for the manager to get to know his staff and for them to get to know each other.
  3. Church staff and membership need time to share their thoughts by going on retreats.
  4. Learn to think like the person with whom you are attempting to build rapport (walk a mile in another man's shoes).
- Keep information about each individual on cards, a hand-held device, or laptop computer.
- Don't judge others too quickly. Sometimes first impressions can be misleading. For example:

A man called a church and asked if he could speak to the head hog at the trough.

The secretary asked, "Who?"

The man replied, "I want to speak to the head hog at the trough!"

Sure that she had heard correctly, the secretary replied, "Sir, if you mean our pastor, you will have to treat him with more respect and ask for 'the reverend' or 'the pastor,' but certainly you cannot refer to him as the head hog!"

The man responded, "I see. Well, I have $10,000 I was thinking about donating to the building fund."

The secretary exclaimed, "Oh my, hold the line, I think the big pig just walked through the door!"

- Learn with whom you are dealing. It may make a difference in the long run!

Chapter 5
The Unspoken Undertow:
Character Really Matters

"Teach the wise, and they will be wiser. Teach the righteous, and they will learn more."
-Proverbs 9:9 (NLT)

"A leader is someone that will take you to the levels of achievement that you want to reach. Leaders inspire their followers to have complcte trust in them. Leaders will never ask more of their followers than they would ask of themselves. Leaders develop leaders and I truly believe that you can't be a good leader without good character."
-Tim Horton, Wide Receiver Coach, Air Force Academy

To lead and create winners, you need a basis of **underlying moral character.**

I love the Okeefeenoke Swamp. This year a friend of mine and I took the boat tour through this intriguing home of hundreds of alligators. I enjoyed the scenery, but I also learned a great deal about the environment. Okeefeenoke means *"land that shakes."* The development of peat beneath the surface of the shallow water of the ocean causes the shaking. As the peat decays, gases build. The build-up periodically forms a "blow-up" of a huge patch of peat which eventually floats to the top and forms land when it dries. You can walk on this patch; however, it is not solid. Of course, this patch looks exactly like the land that is solid, but it shakes when any pressure is applied. This explains its name. Beneath the surface lies a stream of water called an undertow. Webster's dictionary defines an undertow as: "an underlying current, force, or tendency that is in opposition to what is apparent." Character is like the undertow; it is an underlying force.

People whom I have met at the top have that underlying character. In 1995, nearly twenty percent of the Florida's high school juniors and seniors who took the competency test failed.

Another ten percent of the students dropped out before they could even be tested. One of those students demonstrated that character has everything to do with academic achievement. This student grew up in a poor section of Miami. He was an undisciplined teenager who managed to fail most of his classes. In high school he started playing football. His coach drove home the importance of discipline and responsibility during talks with his team. His guidance counselor and teachers taught him that virtue must be practiced in school as well as in sports. Soon, he began to see the classroom as an extension of the playing field. He wanted to compete there and win. Although he studied constantly, he realized that he had an uphill battle to overcome years of underachievement. He took the Scholastic Aptitude Test several times before finally earning a score that would make him eligible for college. For three years, he earned a spot on the All-Academic Team in the Southeastern Conference with a B+ grade point average.

Character counts. People who exhibit strong moral character in their dealings with others whether in sales, sports, churches, or other professions or life in general are those who reach the top of their professions or "make it" in life. Many times their underlying character has placed them way above others in the same field. In today's world, people who have strong character have become harder and harder to find, but character is a fundamental part of leadership. You must show that strong character in order to lead successfully.

Character sustains people during the rough times that all encounter. One of these successful leaders is Coach Mark Richt. His football team at the University of Georgia has reached a new level of success under his leadership because of his strong character and the characters of his assistants. Mark himself teaches a character education class to his team. Dave Van Halanger, the strength and conditioning coach, an integral part of the program at Georgia, inspires kids with character-based strength training.

A person with character by definition possesses moral excellence and firmness. Every single leader that I know realizes the importance of character, even those who have fallen because of not listening to their consciences. Each has taught how to achieve character, has demanded that his/her followers show character, and has lived his/her life with character. That does not mean that he/she does not have character flaws, but it does mean that the teaching and demanding of character is important to obtaining the goals each is trying to reach.

A child's prayer states it well, "God, make all the bad people good and all the good people nice."

When President Jefferson searched for someone to record information about the territory west of the Mississippi River and to make a map of the area, he could not find anyone who met all the requirements: a complete understanding of botany, the natural sciences, and mineralogy, and a familiarity with Native Americans. In his search he stressed the need for that person to have a strong moral character. Since no person met all the requirements, what special quality did Lewis have to make Jefferson choose him? He had a strong moral character.

When a coach talks about a team having character, or a sales manager says the team he works with has character, what exactly does that person mean? First of all, people of character must have morals. They should understand the difference between right and wrong behavior. If you wish to be a strong leader, you should have a code of morals by which you live and by which you model your life. You must do certain things. For example, you must tell the truth; you must work honestly; you must not steal, etc. You must have a strong moral character.

Several leaders of a company asked me to help them draw up a code of ethics for their company. After several meetings of listening to them list their requirements, I simply told them they needed to adopt the Ten Commandments as a code of ethics. They were in agreement until they realized that many of them had already broken that code.

Our culture promotes moral relativism, which says that black or white shouldn't exist, but all should be shades of gray. This belief can cause the downfall of a team or an organization. People must say that they are going to do that because it is the right thing to do. I once heard a pastor say that he knew what the church's bylaws said about the financial policy, but the right thing to do was to pay that person and drop the discussion. I like that.

Although we live in an age of moral relativism, God does have his absolutes. Many have argued against the existence of absolutes, but they have failed to think through to the logical consequences of their positions. If there are no absolutes, then there is no God. If there is no God, then the majority must rule as to what is right or wrong. Whatever people agree to as right becomes right. I hope you can see the fallacy of that position. No one can live for long without agreeing that some absolutes must exist. People of character usually do the right thing because they operate with absolutes! People of character respect other people. I have observed with interest the development of Affirmative Action in companies. I find it interesting that we attempt to legislate morality, but we had to make the attempt because people do not always do the right thing. I wonder what would happen if people treated people fairly and rightly, did the moral thing, and did not use prejudice in deciding what was right or what was wrong? What would happen if we used these absolutes in the hiring and promoting of people?

PC USA

People of character have certain standards that they uphold. Some actions are simply not acceptable to them. The Air Force Academy's underlying code of honor always impresses me. When I speak there, I am aware of the character that overshadows that program. The students simply must respect authority, their fellow students, and others. Their respectful response to teachers and coaches permeates the way they play.

People with character have integrity. Webster's dictionary defines integrity as "soundness, an adherence to a code of moral, artistic or other values." The synonym is honesty. In Shakespeare's *Hamlet,* Polonius sums up the main concept in his advice to Laertes:

> *"...to thine own self be true,*
> *And it must follow, as the night the day,*
> *Thou canst not then be false to any man."*
> (Act 1, Scene iii, Lines 78-80)

Once upon a time, a man's word was his bond. I contend that a time still exists for mankind to exhibit moral fiber and integrity through words and actions. If you do this, you will rise as a leader.

People with character have a polite disposition. They practice manners and show respect and concern for others. The Southeastern Conference has a good-works team that picks athletes

56

who show concern and care for their communities. I have always watched with interest as coaches make athletes perform certain "character acts" like working with Habitat for Humanity, Boy's Clubs, or delivering meals to the needy. Those with character performed similar actions without prompting. At Mississippi State University I visited the ill in hospitals as part of the weekly pre-game activities and often saw guys with character perform the same acts on their own without prompting.

Charlie Ward and Danny Wuerffel, both Hiesman trophy winners, have character that spills out into other people's lives naturally. During their college years, no coach needed to assign them service projects so they would look good in the press. Helping others who ran programs for children and visiting patients in the hospital were things that these two young men had been doing long before the idea of a "good-works team" was born.

Sports writers have written much about Cal Ripken, Junior's phenomenal record of playing in more than 2,500 consecutive baseball games. Although Cal Ripken, Jr. has tremendous talent, he did not set this record as a result only of that talent. His character and his work ethic also allowed him to set it. Many records have been set by players who had a brilliant day, or even a brilliant season, but who didn't have the character to sustain success year-after-year. Cal Ripken, Jr. has had a brilliant career because he has more than talent; he has character.

At the time of the writing of this book, Fellowship of Christian Athletes, coaches, and personnel at universities and colleges across the country have been dealing with gambling and other character issues in the National Collegiate Athletic Association. Most athletic teams are facing character related issues. All great teams are now planning strategies to teach classes on developing character. Many of the team leaders feel that the players need a moral compass to guide them.

To lead you must teach character. How do you teach character in your companies, in your churches, or in your teams, given your time constraints and the diversity of your charges?

- **Set standards on your moral compass.** You as a leader must take the time to discover your personal moral compass. What do you base your value system upon and how do you define that?

You must adopt your own standards to start the process. You must also set standards in the group you are trying to lead.

- **Consider the limitations** on setting standards and implementing them. What does your company, school, or church allow? What are your personnel guidelines and what limitations are placed upon them? Whom can you impose the standards upon? Who makes up your team?

- **Take time to teach standards**. You must teach the standards you have determined. Write these standards down. Put them in understandable, clear, and inoffensive words. Far too many times it seems to me that we do too much assuming of knowledge. Keep a notebook and give copies of it to the people you are leading. In that, specifically list your expectations to help each person understand what they mean. Plan a strategy of teaching those standards.

- **Require standards**. Make sure that you require standards and impose them on the people you teach. I believe in playing offense. Spell out the demand on each person and the consequences if he or she breaks the standards.

- **Have a code of ethics** for your team. Select a representative group from the team and have them assist you in writing a code of ethics and adapt them for the group.

A leader's biggest mistake at the top is what I call "**the assumption factor**!" The leader makes assumptions that should not be made:

- The leader assumes that "everyone knows what he/she believes!" Many of the leaders I have seen at the top think that if they make life-style choices and if they live certain ways that everyone will just know what they believe, but the message often gets lost in translation. A leader unapologetically needs to say at an

58

appropriate time that he/she is not imposing anything on his/her followers, but that he/she wants them to understand where he/she is coming from in making decisions.

- Leaders often assume that the people whom they lead will "do right." I have heard several coaches addressing their teams before a weekend or after a game tell their athletes that they know what is right so they shouldn't get into trouble during the weekend, and I have heard bosses tell their employees that there were certain things that they knew that they just weren't to do. These assumptions are invalid. "What is right" may vary from individual to individual on that team or in that company. Every organization must have a written code of ethics, the standards that members must follow.

- Leaders also assume that nobody wants to be told what to do. People learn certain behaviors. Leaders should teach the expected behavior patterns because far too many people do want instructions and respond to well-stated parameters. I trust that you as a leader will accept the responsibility of teaching a code of ethics.

Having character and being gifted are two entirely different things. Character is doing what is right when no one is around to see.

Maybe all leaders should pray, "May our private thoughts always be as impressive as our public lives; and, whatever our gifts, may they be excelled by excellent character."

Chapter 6
Let's Talk about Personal Responsibility

"If you say, 'But we knew nothing about this,' does not he who weighs the heart perceive it? Does not he who guards your life know it? Will he not repay each person according to what he has done?" -Proverb 24:12 (NIV)

"A leader must stay the course when he is confronted by doubt and fear from within and without. He must have the passion to feel, the perseverance to continue and the will to discipline. A leader must empower those below him to grow by delegation and belief. He must have the confidence and trust to listen to his people and embrace their thoughts and ideas." -Tommy Bowden, Head Football Coach, Clemson University

Every leader must face the **ultimate responsibility** for producing a finished product. Each of us has personal responsibility to develop winners. Leadership begins to happen when you decide that you see the situation. You understand that you are the leader, and you will get it done. These points are things that every leader must say to himself/herself in order to lead well.

The most obvious truth I have discovered at the top is that people who lead have learned to be **responsible**. They do not blame their past, the weather, or the circumstances for their mistakes. They are willing to be responsible for the consequences of these actions. It is what the pastor who really wants to change a church's direction does. It is what a coach who wants the team to become better performers does. It is what a manager who wants to increase sales does. Each simply takes responsibility for the good results **and** the bad results. Each shows acceptance through words and actions. I believe you can make mistakes. You can even be unreliable in some situations and make bad judgments, but you still must never be irresponsible.

Many books on leadership tell the reader how Abraham Lincoln became a successful leader, or how Winston Churchill achieved his position of leadership, or give some other person's method of reaching the top. The problem arises when you try to copy them. Their methods worked for them. You must find your own way. You may use some of the information you have learned from books and from other people, but you must blend that information with your own special qualities. No one can exactly copy someone else. Do your own thing! Be your own person!

Do you remember that great *Peanuts* cartoon about baseball? The first inning is underway and Charlie's team is getting hammered. The score is something like 25-0. Someone suggests that Charlie needs to quit, but Charlie says that he has not yet come to bat! This chapter is the call for you to come to bat.

You must be who you are as Shakespeare's Cassius in *Julius Caesar* reminds you:

> *"Men at some time are masters of their fates*
> *The fault, dear Brutus, is not in our stars,*
> *But in ourselves, that we are underlings."*

(Act I, scene ii, Lines 139-141)

You alone are responsible for your actions. You must suffer or be rewarded by the consequences of your actions.

What is personal responsibility? Get a definition that you can live with and surround it with a plan of action. After you establish your own definition for responsibility, you must understand that whatever else is happening in your family, with your job, or with your team, you are responsible for it. You can make a difference. The more you push yourself and the more you evaluate yourself, the better control you have of the situation. You can make something happen; you can make things work out.

Many of you have met the dream-takers in life and have allowed them to take you hostage to the circumstances in which you find yourself. When I first started working with athletes at Florida State University, I challenged the players by telling them that they could be either a thermometer or a thermostat. I explained that the thermostat sets the temperature in the room while a thermometer simply measures the temperature that has already been set. Your decision to control your situation and not be pressed by it into a mold will make you a leader. When Coach Bowden started at Florida State University, he had inherited a program that historically played second fiddle to the University of Florida. In the early days, especially when it came to recruiting, he got those players whom Florida did not want. But Coach Bowden never let that be the thermometer for what he and his staff could be. He became the thermostat that changed the environment. You too cannot be held captive by the existing circumstances. Become serious about resetting the temperatures. You be the thermostat!

One of my favorite stories tells about a mule that was dearly loved by all. Because of its age, the farmer felt it had outlived its usefulness. The farmer, however, couldn't bring himself to actually shoot it. He decided to simply put the mule down a deep abandoned well and throw dirt on it. Every time dirt came into the well, the mule shook it off and stepped up onto the resulting pile of dirt. He stepped up; shook if off; stepped up; shook it off... before long he was out of the well!

You cannot let the dirt of your situation keep you in the hole either. You must step up and get out of the situation. When you lose your passion and your dream leaves you, you are stuck in mediocrity. The following words are contrary to what most people today think about life, including people in the church. The famous British preacher F.W. Robertson preached these words in a sermon on August 12, 1849:

> Life, like war, is a series of mistakes, and he is not the best Christian or the best general who makes the fewest false steps. Poor mediocrity may secure that; but he is the best who wins the most splendid victories by the revival of mistakes.

Henry Ford, the great auto tycoon, would have agreed with Robertson because Ford defined a mistake as "an opportunity to begin again, more intelligently."

Not only should you learn from your mistakes but you should also strive to live life to its fullest. An unknown author wrote a poem about his wasted chances in life that left him mired in mediocrity.

> *I'm a small and lonely man, my friend,*
> *The world will not build a monument to me,*
> *Somehow I've become sunken*
> *In the mire of mediocrity.*

Alone along life's torturous trail
Repeating my meaningless deeds,
Early errors now haunt me
And like a tumor on me feeds.
Great things left to other men,
Great decisions not my care,
Noble steps and moments
Not my privilege to share.

Each life has its crossroads,
Be careful which you choose,
A life of greatness and happiness
Is all too easy to lose.

People who change the world are those who live above the level of mediocrity. To just get by in today's world is not acceptable to true leaders. They cannot live in a world ruled by mediocrity; they must excel in their fields.

You must choose to take personal responsibility, regardless of the sacrifice, effort required, or the end results. Taking that responsibility is the only way that you can make an impact. Failure to do that is a failure to lead,

Get a grip on the dream and rise above the mediocrity that can hold you captive. When you do, things will change:

- Your life – by this I mean the daily grind. If you take responsibility, you start your day thinking differently. You relate to people with a different attitude. You don't simply think that you are a victim of life. You become the person who really takes control of the situations that you encounter.
- Your marriage – If you are willing to be personally responsible for yourself, you will find a new way to become a part of a team.
- Your relationships – All relationships improve if you accept responsibility for making them work, and if you make an effort to see that they do.
- Your job – If you accept responsibility for your job, the way you behave in that job is set.

The football program at the University of Georgia only gets better as Mark Richt leads there. I always enjoy listening to Mark's call-in show. I remember a time during his first season of coaching at Georgia when he made a mistake in a key game. He made a bad call. A caller to his radio show asked Mark about the call. Mark made a huge impression on me when he told the caller that he had made a bad decision, but if he were given another chance, he would not make the same call. He continued by saying that he hoped that he had learned so that he wouldn't make the same mistake again. Mark did not blame the situation, the circumstances, another coach, or even an immature player. He took personal responsibility for it. His personal acceptance of responsibility makes him a strong leader.

Coach Ken Sparks at Carson Newman makes adjustments easily. He always seems willing to make necessary changes. He spends time trying to figure out a new way to motivate his team. Although they win consistently, he worries about going to the next level. He personally continually evaluates and makes changes in his tactics. He holds himself responsible for his team, so if he needs to make an adjustment in his approach, he does.

Step up to the plate. Your turn at the bat has come. Here are some tools for hitting a homerun instead of striking out. Within these categories you should find the tools you need to become a power hitter.

- Personal Development.
- Persistent Decisions.
- Painful Realities.
- Powerful Surroundings.
- Peculiar Rewards.

Let's talk a little about **personal development**. Leaders at the top work on personal development. A leading pastor in the country, who also is over fifty-five years of age, invited me to attend a conference with him. He simply believes that one must continue to learn and to develop new skills in order to become the best possible leader.

You must examine your life to assess your strengths and weaknesses properly. Your life will not improve if you seldom take personal responsibility. I call the leadership evaluation a "leadership moment." This is the time that all of the necessary things line up for you to have your greatest leadership potential. Your abilities, gifts, experiences, and skills, line up and the moment occurs.

I wish I could say that every job and every pastorate that I have had were in line with my own leadership moments. It never happened. There were some moments when I did an adequate job and others when I did a good job, but there were few electric moments when I did an awesome job. At those times all the items lined up, and I did the best job I possibly could. If you are going to discover the leadership places where you do your best development of leaders, you must perform a good personal evaluation.

Personal evaluation involves checking your **impact on others**. When you meet people, to what part of your personality do people react and respond? Do you have an impact on others, and do they have an automatic reaction to you when you are in a room?

I recently attended a conference in a different field than those to which I am accustomed. I was aware that I was an outsider, but even in their field these people had an impact on me in a negative way. The people were not very warm or outgoing. They tended to gather in cliques.

At one point I looked at a friend who was at the conference with me and asked, "Do you get any vibes here?"

He swiftly answered, "Yeah, I do not see one person with whom I would like to spend time!"

Be careful how you impact others!

Now I know we were hard on that group, but the fact that they had impacted us both in the same way was interesting. I am not sure that all you can do to study your impact on others will help, but you should at least evaluate your behavior style and ascertain how you naturally impact people. Are you an introvert or an extrovert? Do you present yourself well? Are you a person who pays attention to the environment around you? Do you make others feel at ease, or do you make them tense? Good assessment of your talents and gifts helps determine your ability to lead. Too many people do not take the responsibility for the effect they have on people. Often, these same people never take enough notice of what is happening around them to realize that the first impression they make on others impacts their ability to lead in the future. The possibility of **a leadership moment** must include how you impact others.

Secondly, you must evaluate your **skill development**. You will discover the leadership moment when you assess the skills that you have and formulate a plan to develop them. You must have skill development to achieve and lead. You may face the danger of assuming that you have learned all there is to learn. If you assume that you have a handle on everything, you may find yourself with a failure in leadership on your hands. For example, I am not very good with details. I can say that I will just hire someone to take care of this problem, but a time may come when circumstances force me to organize and deal with details. To correct my lack of ability in this area, I can attend a time management seminar, a computer usage clinic, or some other organizational class.

When you work hard and achieve some success, you may find the top to be a dangerous place. You may begin to think that you are successful; therefore, you are good. The success leads you to believe that you have learned all that you need to know. You quit learning and no longer develop new skills. This would be a major mistake. Never stop learning!

I know a pastor who is very good at his job. He has worked hard and arrived at the top of his profession. By all standards, his church is a good one. Attendance is high. His leadership skills and his people skills are good. In fact, his church is hitting on "all cylinders" as some would say. However, as his church has grown, expectation has grown and changed. He must now develop some new skills to stay ahead of his success. He needs some good staff skills. Before the church began to grow, no full-time staff existed, just a part-time staff. He hadn't needed to develop those skills. He has been overwhelmed by the growth. Instead of learning new skills to continue to help his church grow, he has determined to continue in his same pattern of behavior. Unfortunately, he needs some new skills. My hearts aches for him as I see the church begin to grow "sour" on him as a leader. The church has grown to the point where it needs to relocate and build, but because he has refused to develop new skills, he may never get a chance to enjoy the fruits of his labor.

On the other hand, Tom Smiley in Gainesville, Georgia, has done an amazing job in taking a church through a host of changes, not the least of which has been a total restructuring of operation, changing some leadership positions, adding new staff, and completing at least three building programs. Tom wears many hats. He is a strong preacher, a creative person, a great staff organizer, and a fabulous dream-maker, but let me tell you what he does best. He stays in a growing pattern. This man is extremely good at skill development because he reads and listens to others. Tom's ability to grow with the moment has at least partly brought about the success of that great church.

When did you last look at the necessary skills for your designated goals? When have you designed a plan to reach those goals? Do you personally have in place a skills development strategy? I would assume you never think that you know it all; therefore, you must take care of these areas.

Perhaps Coach Bobby Bowden' greatest attribute, even though he is seventy-plus-years-old, is his ability to recruit eighteen-year-olds. He accomplishes this by developing new skills and new approaches to the task, and by maintaining a sharp ability for recognizing and implementing every leadership moment.

I also feel strongly about **character development and faith growth.** Real leaders have in place a strategy that aids them in developing their character and their faith. I am stunned at the number of people without basic plans in place to help them develop their character and increase their faith.

My high school coach would remind us, "The only way you can coast is downhill."

I am acutely aware that many "fly by the seat of their pants" in the area of personal character growth development, but this is a hit or miss way of doing things. Instead, have a strategy in place to develop needed skills.

As a leader, you will also need to have a system of **checks and balances** in place. I was a very young pastor when all of the scandals involving men at the top of electronic evangelism happened. Two of those received much publicity. I do not know them or their circumstances, but they obviously needed some checks and balances in their lives. Because of that lack, each was toppled from his place of power. Soon after all of that publicity, I remember being at a conference led by Tony Campolo. He wanted to know who in our lives checked to make sure that our character and our faith continued growing. I remember saying under my breath that no one was holding me accountable, and I did not have a plan to choose anyone to do so. Then, Campolo suggested that the danger of our falling was equal to that of those two evangelists previously mentioned if we did not have someone monitor us. That comment made me realize that no one should stand alone. Everyone could use an overseer to make sure that he or she continues to grow instcad of stagnating. Let me encourage you to find someone to hold you accountable for your growth and character.

Dr. Martin Lloyd Jones, an outstanding pastor, once said, "The worst thing that can happen to some is to succeed before they are ready!"

Real leaders at the top take seriously the need to grow personally.

People at the top do not come to a leadership moment without evaluating their character and faith and without growing on a regular basis in those areas. I wish to tell you about a man who has lost his way. Let's not use his name, but he may be the most powerful person I have ever met in leadership. He has worked hard to make his company a tremendous success. His people skills can take your breath away. He creatively works diligently at organizational skills. However, his personal life has become a moral failure. He has lost his marriage and his direction morally. Though he is hanging on to his company, he is in a battle. He needs someone to be his moral compass to help him find his way.

I would be amiss if I did not say that the need to deal with morality and character is essential to survival. If you are in a leadership position and experience a moral failure, as in the previous case, the situation can be saved. You must simply admit your failure, show remorse, and tell key people in your life that you intend on making amends. In faith, it is called **repentance**. It is essential in a leader. People respect honesty and respond to a person's desire to change.

Proper growing of people skills is the next area where a personal **leadership moment** occurs. It is here that your personal responsibility is enhanced.

If you want to take responsibility for your leadership, you must develop the manner in which you relate to people. This is the age of generation X. You must relate to them in a unique way. Its members fear being alone because so many of them were latchkey children, either because both parents worked or they were the children of single parents. Most of them look for that situation that I call the "Cheers reality." Do you remember the TV show about the Cheers Bar in Boston? One of the lines in the theme song echoes in my mind, "I want to go where everyone knows my name." People like personal attention! I do not care how much you grow or how high up the ladder you climb, if you fail to develop the people skills that recognize that people have value, you will never lead them. You are responsible for developing and using those skills.

We have talked about personal development as a key component of leadership; now let's come to grips with another area where personal responsibility manifests itself: **persistent decisions** that we make every day. These decisions must reflect your core being. As each day begins, no one needs to worry about what you are up to. You are up to it all the time.

Someone suggested that the best way to get anywhere is to start every day with a decision to go there! If you want to achieve a certain goal, begin the needed steps.

Don Pratt, the pastor of First Baptist Church in Tucker, Georgia, has made a commitment to making his church say something to the real world. He wants to cross the bridge from religion to a vital faith in the minds of the people he pastors. For much too short a time, he was my pastor and I served on his staff. Over the time that I have known him, we have had many lunches and talked many times on the phone. His effort to make the church plug into the real world begins each workday. He thinks of ways to make his commitment happen. It permeates his every move, his every discussion. His plan works this way: When he gets to work, he is focused on accomplishing that plan. His dealings with everyday decisions, his reading, and his Internet surfing all point him in that direction.

You must decide about every part of your dream every day of your life. Bobby Bowden will never walk away from the desire to be the best coach of the best team in the country. Tommy Bowden is no different than his father. He manifests his thoughts, his strategy, and his plans all day long, beginning at the start of the day. Persistent deciding is the only way dreams stay alive!

You must persistently decide about priorities. Focus on your priorities, but, at the same time, allot your time wisely. It is not enough to think about it; you must do certain things each day to make it happen.

Steve Brown leads my list of successful pastors. Steve has been my friend for a long time. When he preaches, he makes the sermon leap into your life. His priority is teaching the Bible. So guess what he prepares to do every day? He chooses his subject and connects it to the Bible. While out and about, he listens to everyone's stories and makes notes. He reads and writes that information down because he may be able to connect it to a story in the Bible. He makes a persistent decision to do that every day.

Persistent daily decisions are made by those at the top about time to be spent, about reactions to be solicited, and about tasks to be accomplished. You do not get to the top unless you make those decisions persistently.

Painful realities need to be considered if you take personal responsibility. You must have some discipline in order to reach the top. You need, just as everyone I have met at the top did, to make a decision and daily stick to it. The discipline of sticking with a task while others might be doing something more interesting is a painful reality. You must have a discipline of time management. You need to stay at the top of your game in your field by reading and listening to tapes, going to seminars, attending lectures, as well as talking with those who can help you do your job better. This is the discipline of focus or staying with a task. Often these disciplines are painful realities, but you will not do well if you do not have the discipline to achieve.

For example, I am not at the top of my golf game. I might say that I want to play golf, but, I can assure you, I do not incorporate the necessary discipline in my life to improve my game. If I really wanted to be a better player, I would practice. That old adage is true, "Practice makes perfect!" However, I don't have the discipline to practice, so I must accept that I will never to a good golfer.

I will forever remember the day I said to a very talented pianist that I wished I could play a piano as well as he did.

He responded abruptly, "No, you don't!"

I replied, "I really do!"

He returned, "Then you need to practice five hours a day as I do."

Whoa! I thought I really don't want to do that. Discipline is a painful reality, but it is a necessary part of being a winner and a leader.

Not everybody is going to like what you dream. Critics abound. If you dream, you need to expect some criticism. Not everyone is going to like your dream. I remember telling a cousin that I wanted to impact the world by preaching and teaching. He, in no uncertain words, told me the silliness of leaving Mississippi to do something so foolish. You can never please everyone. You must try to please yourself. You cannot lead or be a winner if you listen to the critics. I wonder how many people were in favor of Tommy Bowden's taking his first head-coaching job at Tulane, a school traditionally not known as a powerhouse in football. He learned by following his father's example. Bobby Bowden had chosen to go to Florida State University at a time when the administration was considering dismantling the program because the record was so poor. Those I have met at the top don't listen to critics. They stay focused.

You will encounter disappointments. That's one of life's painful realities. I heard the story years ago about an in incident in the life of actor Kevin Costner. The movie *Silverado* launched Kevin Costner's acting career. But first he had to weather a huge disappointment. After completing his role in *The Big Chill,* Lawrence Kasdan, the film's director, called Costner into his office to explain that he felt terrible, but the length of the film had forced him to cut a scene from the movie eliminating Costner's speaking part. All that was left were a few glimpses of Costner as a corpse. However, this cut did not harm Costner's acting career. Kasdan later made up for those cuts by casting Costner in his first important movie role.

Disappointments happen in all lives, even in the lives of people at the top. Sometimes people whom you count on disappoint. Other times the outcome of a project disappoints. Often dreams don't pan out. You should remember the old adage, "Every cloud has a silver lining." Try to use any negative happenstance as a learning experience.

A dear friend and very successful pastor of a large church has had three staff members involved in moral indiscretions. It would have been so easy for him to change churches and move on, but not this warrior of the faith. He simply sat back, reassessed his hiring practices, and focused more than ever on his goal.

Charles Roesel, my pastor at First Baptist Church of Leesburg, Florida, has done the most incredible job of turning a church around. Charles came to a church that was racially segregated, traditional, and struggling with making an impact on the community. I have watched over the past twenty-five years as he has caused this church to explode in growth and in ministry. Not only have some racial barriers been broken but also the religious system has been revamped to create a church that ministers daily to hundreds in a free medical clinic, a rescue mission, a women's shelter, and many other ministries. Charles experienced disappointments in attitudes, failures, and trivial fighting, but his heartfelt need to achieve his goal for the church has never stopped. This great church has become the premier church in the Southern Baptist Convention in Ministry Evangelism.

Never underestimate the **importance of powerful surroundings**. The people I have met at the top have a great secret I want to reveal to you: **They hang around other people who dream**. They work and spend time with other people at the top so they learn from one another. For example, the Amway (Quixtar) people each year have what they call the "Diamond Club," an organization of the people who have succeeded at what they do within the company. Watch the great coaches of football in America come together at the Nike convention. It is a great trip, but they learn from each other as well. Willow Creek Community Church in the Chicago area, Saddleback Church in California, and North Point Community Church in the Atlanta area all host conferences for people who want to be around successful people in their fields.   Successful people want to spend time with other successful people. They want to learn from people who are at the top.

I like to check out the reading materials, especially the books, of successful people when I visit in their homes or offices. After exploring their libraries, I find that coaches, sales people, pastors, and others at the top read some of the same books, go to some of the same websites, and even go to some of the same conferences.

I find that not only do successful people hang around some of the same people, but also they go to the same places that support dreams. Besides conferences, they even vacation in some of the same places. They love "thinking places" and "front-porch kind" of places that rekindle their hearts and help them keep the dream flowing in their minds. I remember being at a conference with pastor and writer Stu Weber and asking him to recommend a place to stay in the Seattle, Washington area. Without missing a beat, he said that he knew just the place, one where you can catch your breath while sitting on the front porch. I followed his advice. I vividly remember the day I, too, sat on that front porch, caught my breath, and had a very creative day.

I have also noticed that people at the top have **supportive people in their lives**. My friend Ed Knickman, a successful man in a networking business, is married to Rose. She is a compliment to everything he does. She epitomizes the supporting role of a leader's mate. She, in her own right, is a strong person, but she compliments every character glitch he has.

Pastor Steve Cloud runs the show and leads a large congregation, but his wife Trish compliments the areas that need to be shored up. Even their children get into the act.   Another example is the Pratt family. Don and Cindy Pratt actually pastor the church at Tucker, Georgia, but their daughters cast visions there as well.

Have you seen Ann Bowden, Bobby's wife and Tommy's mother, interviewed on television when her husband squares off against her son in the annual Bowden Bowl between Florida State University and Clemson University? She is a genius in showing support for her husband while not being unsupportive toward her son. She is a compliment to both.

Maybe one of the most interesting negative stories I have ever heard concerns a trip that the managers of a major company made with their top sales people. These people had made a great deal of money for their company and had been outstanding in the production of a profit. The company, to reward them, flew them to a resort area noted for its ambience. When they and their spouses arrived, no one introduced them to one another, to the "top brass," or to the other spouses. No one gave any special recognition, no applause, no mention of their accomplishments, no presentation of plaques, and no time spent shaking hands with those who had worked so hard. Spouses who had relinquished time with mates so they could work all those hours to make all those goals never visited with the president or the managers. Needless to say, it did not look like an atmosphere that encouraged leadership and winners. This was a major failure for this company and a waste of money. This wasted time could have been used as a bonding experience. People could have hung around and learned from others, swapped ideas, and experienced encouragement, but these things just didn't happen. This was tragic but far too typical in today's world.

A part of the journey to the top motivates you to accept personal responsibility. The journey itself teaches. In college football one of the toughest roles is that of a "walk-on" player, someone who has decided to play college football with no guarantee of a scholarship. He has a rough road ahead. Honestly, not many people make it. I remember many conversations over the years with walk-on athletes who were thinking seriously about walking away from the attempt. When they came to me, their chaplain, to ask for help, I could tell them that they had a great chance to make it, or I could tell them the truth. I learned that truth was good! However, I did tell them that often the trip itself would be worth the price. The experiences with the team whether they received a scholarship or not, would make them better people. They could tell their children and their grandchildren they had played ball, and they could be a part of something bigger than themselves. Sometimes we get **peculiar rewards** because the reward isn't always what we want or expect.

If you are going to take personal responsibility for your life and your success, the journey is worth it. I would rather attempt something great and fail than never try. This book may well be the illustration of that concept. I will have tried even if I do not make it to Oprah's show!

Financial rewards are certainly a strong motivation for attempting great things. I would never forget that. Most people who have made it to the top have found a reward for that in a financial way. Though that is true, in my experience, many at the top who are personally responsible see money as a side issue.

The last thing that I would mention as a reward for personal responsibility is the **personal satisfaction**. For me, it is the "sitting on the porch late in the afternoon feeling" I get when I have finished a task.

As I write this chapter, I am sitting at a desk in Virginia at a bed-and –breakfast near Lexington. What a marvelous place to be! I will come back here and write again. The area is rich in history. Robert E. Lee and Stonewall Jackson both lived here. I enjoy the history and will treasure what I have learned. Yesterday afternoon my wife and I sat on the porch assessing our lives. We have recently consulted with a financial adviser about retiring soon or at least taking social security. As I sat there, I talked with my wife Donnelle about a sense of accomplishment. I have a lot of personal satisfaction in where I have been and cannot wait to see where I will end. This personal satisfaction has been a strong motivator in my life, as it has been in the lives of all the people whom I have met at the top.

I am not especially fond of poetry, but I like the following poem because it says all I have tried to say in this chapter. A missionary in attendance at a session of senior adults who were finishing the race gave me the poem. It says it all! Again.

A Psalm of Life

Tell me not in mournful numbers,
Life is but an empty dream!
For the soul is dead that slumbers,
And things are not what they seem.

Life is real! Life is earnest!
And the grave is not its goal;
'Dust thou art, to dust returnest,'
Was not spoken of the soul.

Not enjoyment, and not sorrow,
Is our destined end or way;
But to act, that each to-morrow
Find us further than to-day.

"Art is long, and Time is fleeting,
And our hearts, though stout and brave,
Still, like muffled drums, are beating
Funeral marches to the grave.

In the world's broad field of battle,
In the bivouac of Life,
Be not like dumb, driven cattle!
Be a hero in the strife!

Trust no Future, howe'er pleasant!
Let the dead Past bury its dead!
Act – act in the living Present!
Heart within, and God o'erhead!

Lives of great men all remind us
We can make our lives sublime,
And, departing, leave behind us
Footprints on the sands of time;

Footprints, that perhaps another,
Sailing o'er life's solemn main,
A forlorn and shipwrecked brother,
Seeing, shall take heart again.

Let us, then, be up and doing,
With a heart for any fate;
Still achieving, still pursuing,
Learn to labour and to wait.

Henry Wadsworth Longfellow

Chapter 7
Carpe Mañana

"A wise youth works hard all summer; a youth who sleeps away the hour of opportunity brings shame."
-Proverbs 10:5 (NLT)

"A leader inspires, motivates, plants a vision into his/her followers, trains and encourages them to do things they don't like to do in order to accomplish the ultimate goal. A confident and courageous leader follows the Jesus model of servant leadership and inverts the pyramid in team building so no one cares who gets the credit, as long as the mission is accomplished." -Dal Shealy, President, Fellowship of Christian Athletes

When writing about leadership, the people at the top "seize tomorrow!" They are not bothered by change, paradigm shifts, or tough times. They simply seize the situation and push through it. These leaders grasp opportunities when presented, "do life" better, adapt to change in the environment, enlarge their backyards, decide what matters in life, use their brains, have the courage of their convictions, develop their listening habits, build character, and have a belief in the goodness of others. To be a good leader you too must seize tomorrow by following these guidelines.

For example, many people watched to see how Coach Tommy Bowden would handle Clemson's loss to Wake Forest during the 2003 season since that loss would put his job in jeopardy. I asked him what his plans were. He told me he felt that he probably had to beat Florida State University to save his job. You would think with that challenge in front of him, he would have devised a way to get out gracefully. Not this guy. He seized the opportunity and set out to do his thing. He beat Florida State University and kept his job! He had seized tomorrow and accomplished what he set out to do!

Andy Stanley and his staff started a church in Atlanta that would become a most exciting church at a time when starting a church outside denominational lines was a risk. Today, North Point Community Church is a beacon of creativity. Andy took a look at the environment surrounding him and decided that he could accomplish more outside the normal parameters. He seized tomorrow! The church is exploding!

You must **grasp each opportunity** that arises. This concept is illustrated by the story of a young soldier and his commanding officer who get on a train together. The only available seats are across from an attractive young lady who is traveling with her grandmother. As they engage in pleasant conversation, the soldier and the young lady keep eyeing one another. There is an obvious mutual attraction. Suddenly the train goes into a tunnel and the compartment becomes dark. Immediately, two sounds are heard —the "smack" of a kiss and the "whack" of a slap across the face.

The grandmother thinks, "I can't believe he kissed my granddaughter, but I'm glad she gave him the slap he deserved."

The young girl thinks, "I'm glad he kissed me, but I wish my grandmother hadn't slapped him for doing it."

The commanding officer thinks, "I don't blame the boy for kissing the girl, but it's a shame that she missed his face and hit me instead."

As the train breaks into the sunlight, the soldier cannot wipe the proud smile off his face. He has just seized the opportunity to kiss a pretty girl and slap his commanding officer, and he has gotten away with both!

Once we were taught to carpe diem—seize the day, but if you only seize today, it will be gone before you know it. Instead, we need to talk about how you as a leader can carpe mañana— seize tomorrow. How can you seize tomorrow?

- Get a better grip on your life.
- Just "do life."
- Get a handle on a plan to improve in "doing life."

I want to help you get a grip on life. "Do life" better!

"Doing life better" will require more self examination than you often choose to do for fear that you will look ridiculous. But I have concluded that you can be whatever you choose to be as long as you are willing to take stock of what you are trying to be on a regular basis. Maybe you need to ask yourself what to do. Do you want to be a leader? Are you willing to do what is necessary to get there? Can you make sacrifices to achieve your goal? Can you be a role model or person of character? Does your life have a purpose? Can you focus on the important things and forget the trivial? Can you allow God to be a part of your life?

A difficult task is **adapting to change**. Someone has said in this age you are either making history or you are history. There was an anonymous poem going around the Internet sometime ago that speaks to that idea.

Not so long ago...
An application was for employment
A program was a TV show.
A cursor used profanity.
A keyboard was a piano!
Memory was something you lost in old age.
A CD was a bank account,
And if you had a 3-½ inch floppy you hoped no one found out!

Compress was something you did to garbage
Not something you did to a file!
And if you unzipped anything in public
You'd be in jail for a while!

Log on was adding wood to a fire.
Hard drive was a long trip on the road.
A mouse pad was where a mouse lived,
And backup was what happened to your commode!

Cut you did with a pocket knife.
Paste you did with glue.
A web was a spider's home,
And a virus was the flu!

I guess I'll stick to my pad and paper,

And the memory in my head.
I hear nobody's been killed in a computer crash,
But when it happens they wish they were dead!

Whether you like it or not you are all immigrants in a www.com world, and your kids can get around in it better than you can. You are migrants from a manual world in an age of the computer and the cell phone and faxes! Change with the times. Learn to use these instruments to aid you.

When I was growing up, the sexiest woman that I knew on television was Mary Tyler Moore. Today people think a realistic survivor on the show *Survivor* or a contestant on *The Bachelor,* who will marry a bachelor for a million dollars, is sexy. No wonder people look for love in all the wrong places; there are so many wrong places.

How do you do it? How do you seize tomorrow in this kind of world? Work from a larger parameter. **Enlarge your backyard**. I love the story of the teacher telling all the children in her third grade class to go home, sit in their backyards, and count the stars when they came out. Then the next day they were to come to class and share what they had seen. She thought it would teach them about the number of stars and large numbers. The next day she asked Mary how many stars she had seen. Mary's answer was simple. She said that she had seen about 1,000 stars and then could not count any more. Suzy had seen 1,201. Then the teacher asked Johnny how many he had seen. He said that he had seen 112. The teacher was astonished and asked him why he had not seen more. In his mind, the answer was simple. He told the teacher that maybe some backyards were bigger than others!

I honestly believe the enlarging of your backyard and getting a vision for what you can be are the beginnings of being a leader and producing winners.

Many coaches in schools across America have large backyards. One of these is Jimmy Scroggins, a high school football coach at Bay High School in Panama City, Florida. He is at the top in everyway. Jimmy's backyard has always been bigger than just coaching a high school team. He uses his large backyard for instilling character traits in young men. Another fine coach Brad Lane works in a small high school in Vidalia, Georgia. Even though his actual geographical area is small, I can assure you that in this tiny little town, Brad has a big backyard. He uses all of it to influence people daily.

As you get older, your vision should improve. Not your vision of earth, but your vision of heaven. Those who have spent their lives looking for heaven gain a skip in their steps as that city comes into view.

After Michelangelo died, someone found in his studio a piece of paper on which he had written a note to his apprentice. In the handwriting of his old age, the great artist had written, "Draw, Antonio, draw, and do not waste time."

That was well-founded urgency, Michelangelo. Time slips. Days pass. Years fade, and life ends. What you came to do must be done while there is time!

Some of you play in the same small backyards that you have always inhabited because your will and your way do not search for larger spaces. These things make you selfish. Some of you:

- Play in the small yard of today which usually makes you plan poorly and never look toward the future.
- Play in the small yard of making money which gives you the wrong priorities in life.
- Play in the small yard of pleasure and use people.
- Play in the small yard of hurt past so you never get to enjoy the present and the future.
- Play in the small yard of rational thinking so you never enjoy dreaming of the impossible.

Many play in small yards; therefore, their vision is limited. For you to become a leader who produces winners, you must widen your space. Enlarge your backyard.

Pick a number, any number. Did you pick a number larger than a million? If you didn't, why didn't you? Larry Page and Sergey Brin founded Google, an Internet search engine. The word googol is a mathematical term for the number one followed by one hundred zeroes. While most people are likely to pick a number like fourteen or ninety-eight, Page and Brin decided to pick a googol.

Internet users perform one hundred million plus searches a day on Google. How did Google get so big? I don't have the expertise to answer that question, but I can tell you that it began with their initial vision. They thought large, so the response was large.

Enlarge your backyard. Please, enlarge your yard!

Use your brain. Competence is the ability to think about things that matter and ignore the things that don't!

Decide what matters. Learning what you are competent at doing and concentrating on that competence is the way you get things done. People usually try to prove themselves by doing everything they can even though they sometimes cannot do everything well. Eliminate spending your time doing things you do not do well. Delegate.

- **Use your brain to** assess properly to what you need to give your passion. It is all right to try things and then stop and try others. Often people make life a ball game, and if they strike out on a project, they do not know how to say that doesn't work for them. They have a tremendous amount of guilt. Don't do that. Use your brain.
- Use your brain to learn what you need to know to do whatever you want to do. Read a book or two, listen to a tape, search the internet, or learn from others the things that will help you do your job better. "Flying by the seat of your pants" is costly.
- Use your brain to find friends that can give you good advice, such as mentors, accountability partners, coaches, or whatever you want to call them. Listen and learn from them about the way you use your time, and how you sell yourself.

In 1955 at the age of seventy-six, Albert Einstein died of an aneurysm. Dr. Thomas Harvey, a Princeton pathologist who did the autopsy, kept Einstein's brain for scientific study He conducted every conceivable test and concluded it was normal in weight and size! The only difference seemed to be that Einstein used his! Maybe that is the place where you need to start! **Use your brain!**

Be the leader you would follow. Sometimes leaders can forget that they are working with people who like to be appreciated, noticed and appreciated.

As shown in the following story, have the **courage of your convictions**. Dr. Evan O'Neill Kane, the chief surgeon of Kane Summit Hospital in York City, was convinced that general anesthesia was too risky for many operations. He believed that people should be operated on with simply a well-administered local anesthesia so the risks of general anesthesia could be by passed.

He was anxious to prove his theory, but he could not find anyone to be a guinea pig to go under the knife while conscious. People were afraid of the feeling returning while under the scalpel.

Finally he found a subject. Kane had performed appendectomies thousands of times. The patient was prepped and brought to the operating room. The local anesthesia was carefully administered, and the surgery began. As always, Kane cut across the right side of the abdomen and went in. He tied the blood vessels, removed the appendix, and sutured the incision.

Remarkably, the patient felt little discomfort. In fact, he was up and about the next afternoon which was remarkable since this was 1921, when people with appendectomies were usually kept in the hospital for at least six days or longer.

This was a milestone in the world of medicine. It was also a display of courage because the patient and the doctor were one and the same! Dr. Kane had operated upon himself!

When I think of the people that I have known that are successful leaders, they have the courage of their convictions. They operate on themselves often. They are fun to be with. They do good things for their friends and non-friends. They are compassionate beings who deal with life with humor, gentle concern, kindness, and courage.

Develop your listening habits. Wise men listen; fools are too busy to hear.

In *Proverbs* in the Bible, Solomon, the wisest man in the world writes about the importance of counsel:

"Let the wise listen and add to their learning,
and let the discerning get guidance."
-Proverbs 1:5 (NIV)

"The way of a fool seems right to him, but a wise
man listens to advice." -Proverbs 12:15 (NIV)

"Plans fail for lack of counsel, but with many
advisers they succeed." -Proverbs 15:22 (NIV)

"Listen to advice and accept instruction, and in the
end you will be wise." -Proverbs 19:20 (NIV)

How do you learn if you do not listen to the people with
whom you meet? You can be influential in a person's life
without being a person of influence. Scott Adams, the creator of
the popular *Dilbert* cartoon told how the people who most
influenced him were not even aware of the things that they taught
him. For example, when he was striving to become a syndicated
cartoonist, he sent his work to cartoon editor after cartoon editor
and received rejection after rejection. One critic even suggested
that he take art lessons. Finally he was offered a contract, but
after so many rejections he could not believe the offer was real.
He wanted to know what he had to change to get the contract.
The editor told him he was good enough already. That
confidence in his ability gave him confidence in himself. A
funny thing happened as a result of Adams' listening. His
drawing improved.

Build your life on something that lasts longer than a
throwaway water bottle –**character**.

The psalmist in the Bible wrote:

*"Oh, the joys of those who do not follow the advice of the
wicked,*
Or stand around with sinners,
Or join in with scoffers.
But they delight in doing everything the Lord wants;

day and night they think about his law.
They are like trees planted along the riverbank,
*   bearing fruit each season without fail.*
Their leaves never wither,
*   and in all they do, they prosper. "*
-Psalms 1:1-3 *(*NLT)

"How can a young person stay pure?
*   By obeying your word and following its rules*
I have tried my best to find you---don't let me wander
*   from your commands. .*
I have hidden your word in my heart, that I might not sin
*   against you. "*   *-Psalms* 119:9-11 (NLT)

Ozzie Smith, a fifteenth-time National League All-Star and considered by many to be the greatest shortstop of all time, is a man of character. He was inducted into the Baseball Hall of Fame on July 28, 2002. In his acceptance speech, he compared his journey to the construction of a baseball:

...Protecting the cork center of this ball and reinforcing it are two distinct rubber shells ... For me these two layers reflect two vital and affirming shells of my core dream. The first shell is my faith in God. With him, I have everything. Without him, I have nothing. The second shell is the faith I had in myself which came through my mother's love and encouragement.... The power of those two shells has been life-sustaining throughout my entire career. Like with a baseball, these shells add enforcement to the core. Without either of them, I would never have completed the journey. One gave me strength, and the other gave me purpose.

The second part of the construction of this baseball is manufactured by the wrapping of over 200 yards of wool around the core.... I see that this is the second critical part of my journey. I refer to it as the Strands of Love and Faith. Strands of Love and Faith that so many other people have wrapped around Ozzie Smith as a person and wrapped around my dream through their love and faith in me....I will never forget the faith that my high school coach, Art

Webb who has passed on, had in me…. Just about the time I was questioning my ability and expressed thoughts of going home, Art got wind of my feelings, called me up, and sternly told me, 'Oz, you're not going to quit. You're going to hang in there and weather the storm!' Because of that call and his faith in me…, I stayed. A simple strand of faith in me helped keep my dream alive.

Be the leader that you would follow. Be a person of character.

Chapter 8
Check List for Leaders

"If you plot evil, you will be lost; but if you plan well, you will be granted unfailing love and faithfulness."
-Proverbs 14:22 (NLT)

"A good leader establishes the direction he will lead and then takes the first step in that direction. He implements the principles to achieve the mission as well as establishes an atmosphere that makes others want to join him. He is a good listener. He recognizes the value of all team members and their particular talents. He delegates authority, which promotes team chemistry by allowing all team members an opportunity to contribute to the success of the team. He sets the standards for servitude, loyalty, honesty, trust and work ethic. By setting these levels of expectation, the leader can now feel content in any successes the organization experiences while the membership can enjoy the fruits of their labor and the feeling that comes with a job well done." -Bob Sanders, Defensive Assistant Coach, Green Bay Packers

Sometimes in my travels I do not fly commercial airlines because of a time factor. On those occasions, I fly in private planes. When I started to fly non-commercially, I knew I had to find some people I could trust with my life. I searched until I found two men who fit the bill: Tim Key and Len Strozier. They are both great pilots who have become good friends. They try to help people like me out of jams and help us get some of our days back. I love to fly with them.

Both of them are extremely cautious about flying. They don't take risks. Their flight pre-plan fascinates me. They both have either a notebook or hand held device with a long **checklist**. They do not fly or even start the engine until they go through the entire checklist. Then before they begin the flight, they have another checklist they consult. I like that because I feel secure flying with these guys every time. All well-planned leaders do the same thing.

Everyone I run into at the top has a list of things he/she does all the time. All day every day each goes by that list and gets things done. Bobby Bowden keeps a notebook in which he notes all-important thoughts that have occurred to him during the day. He frequently consults the notebook to see that he is doing what he planned. You, as a good leader, must make a practice of the same procedure, so you do not forget any important action, reaction, thought, or impression that occurs.

I know an outstanding sales manager who carries a checklist in his daily planner to make sure that he does certain things every day. By doing this he knows exactly what he needs to pay attention to every day. You also need to use reminders or memos; call them what you want. The failure to plan to do certain things will cause you to lose touch with the direction you wish to go. The consequences of a lost thought could be dangerous. What I am proposing is that every day you have a checklist that guides you on the journey of leading.

A teenage boy went into a candy store and bought three boxes of candy. The owner of the store asked why he needed three boxes of candy. The boy explained that he had a blind date with a girl. He wanted all three boxes for her. He planned to give her the five-dollar box of candy if she remembered his name. If she let him hold her hand, he would produce the ten-dollar box. However, if he got to kiss her, he planned to give her the fifteen-dollar box. After his purchases, he went to the girl's house. Since he was early, the girl's father invited him to dinner. The father asked the young man to say thanks before the meal. The boy prayed for about an hour.

Later outside, the confused girl asked, "Why didn't you tell me that you were so religious?"

The boy replied, "Why didn't you tell me your father owned a candy store!"

The moral is that you really need **to get a handle on things**. Know yourself and know the situation. The most comfortable creative leaders have a real **understanding of themselves**.

90

I got a call recently from a very bright young minister who had a serious dilemma on his hands. He had done a good job as a member of a church staff, but the time had come for a change. Change can often cause problems. After making the decision to change, he had to deal with all the offers that he had received. Two were very good offers, each of which would present him with a great ministry opportunity. He asked me for my input.

I began by asking him in what size town he wished to live? I asked what style worship he preferred? I asked whether he felt strongly about the staff having a close relationship or not? I asked about his long-term goals? I went on to tell him that everyone makes decisions about which direction to go based on who he/she is.

One of the newscasters for CNN when reporting upon President Ronald Reagan's death credited the following description to his wife Nancy Reagan, "Ronnie was comfortable inside of his skin!"

Great leaders are comfortable with themselves. They know who they are and where their comfort zones are. They know the place they fit well and places they do not fit well.

Sometimes, I have seen good people in the wrong places. The pairing was poor. Sometimes you choose to go to an unsuitable place for all the wrong reasons instead of letting God choose where you should go.

You, as a leader, need to take a **personality assessment** of some type and have an accountability partner who will give you input about your nature. Also ask that person to help you evaluate yourself and get a handle on just who you are.

Force yourself to look at what you do well and what you do poorly. You must make a proper assessment of your gifts and your skills so you may become a great leader and function well as that leader. You need to chart your weaknesses as well as your strengths.

I have come to understand over the years that I have some behavioral characteristics that need some attention. To compensate for my weakness, I try to hire people on my staff who can counterbalance my weaknesses. For example, Charles Fulton worked with me at Tallahassee. His strength balanced the areas in which I was deficient. I have learned through the years that it takes healthy people who are comfortable with themselves to allow the constant and honest evaluation of themselves as people, but you must do this.

I am amazed that we do things over and over again and continue to fail, without working on **self-improvement**. Some peoples' definition of insanity, "Doing the same things over and over again and expecting to get different results," is applicable. People's lack of preparation constantly surprises me. Over the years I have taught at churches, sales conventions, and coaching clinics. Often I watch as participants attend without any tools to take notes. However, the great leaders come to the sessions with notebooks or tape recorders in their hands. They have come to learn. At one of the clinics of the American Football Coaches Convention, I looked down at the front row to see some of the great coaches in the business looking like rookies as they took notes while many of the new young guys were out in the halls swapping stories instead of attending the sessions to learn what they could.

Carson Newman College holds a coaching clinic for coaches and their wives each spring in Gatlinburg, Tennessee. I love the clinic and think the line-up of clinicians there are some of the best in the country. It attracts the best high school coaches in the southeast. I will never forget seeing the late Nick Hyder, the coach with the most high school wins in the nation, sitting with a pad in hand taking notes when I was teaching people skills. He had come to learn. Bob Sanders, who is retired from Tennessee high schools and now coaches in Georgia, treats each session in the clinics as a new chance to learn. He is developing his skills and asking questions everyday. These same outstanding coaches came to me and asked what they could do to make their teams better. They took my ideas and applied them to their personal situations. The veterans were the ones who were making practical use of the information instead of some of the young coaches who really could have learned from the sessions.

People at the top evaluate themselves and develop their skills. To become that type of leader you must **assess your team**. Who are they and how do they function?

You need to know something of their experiences on a daily basis. How can you manage to teach or to sell a vision to people about whom you know little? I mentioned this before in the section on preparing your checklist. It helps to have at least some knowledge of their families, their hobbies, and their passions. Know the people, events, and music that are important to them.

I do some work with a company that extensively uses voice mail communications. I mentioned during a management seminar class that my sending the same worded voice mail to every person I manage would be a mistake. Instead, I send a different voice mail to everyone in my group. In this case that means I would send twelve voice mails. The immediate response from most of the managers was that they do not have the time for that. They felt their time would be better spent in other ways. However, some of the managers attempted to put my idea into practice. One of them found out what music each of the members of his team liked. When he sent a weekly evaluation of work to each, he played that person's favorite song in the background. Interestingly, he became the leader in his region in sales before the year was over.

The most important room I saw in the home of one head coach I visited was a huge game room. He invited his team to hang out there on weekends during the spring. While the young men were there, he learned much about them. Later he used that knowledge to great effect in his coaching.

A successful business leader takes fishing trips and invites men that work in his warehouse to fish with him. During these trips, he learns about the interests of each. No wonder he is so successful in his business. His people trust him a great deal because he knows who they are.

Manage by walking around. I have read in several places of the importance of knowing where people work and seeing the location. If you are going to give orders to a person, at least know where he or she is when they receive the instructions. The simple idea of walking down the hall to talk with an employee communicates a lot of understanding.

Do you give your people permission to succeed by telling them what you expect? Do you give them the resources and the basic instructions about how and why, so they can succeed? Use the following ideas to help your people succeed:

- Verbally explain. Give permission to make it happen. Too often people fail to give their employees, teams, or congregation permission to make things happen. They use negative feedback instead of positive. Praise your people. Tell them they can go as far as they wish if they try hard enough.

- Constantly reinforce. Tell stories about others who have succeeded. Encourage. Raise the boundaries. Continually praise, but in an honest manner.
- Put your plan into effect. Give your people opportunities to succeed.
- Demand that they live up to their potential. Make succeeding their responsibility. Demand success.
    - First, demanding success puts people where they belong and not in some unsuitable job.
    - Second, demanding success makes people responsible.
    - Third, demanding success focuses people on results instead of effort.

The fundamental principle of leadership is **trusteeship.**

You as a leader should check every day to see if your basic ideals are implemented. You need to see if the little things have been done to assure that you are trusted. Check to see if actions exhibit integrity, character, and concern to their fullest possibilities. If your followers trust you, they will give you permission to lead.

You should check the final item on your list to see if your **passion is in gear**. Steve Cloud, one of my dearest friends, pastors a great church in West Columbia, South Carolina. I once had the pleasure of serving on his staff as he led that great church in a relocation process. Steve goes about his job with the greatest passion I have observed at the top! His passion for what he does is almost over the top! The Greeks often asked at a death if the person had lived with passion. I tell you Steve will die well if that is the qualification. Passion is a part of his personality. His passion is an end result of his life experiences and certainly his faith.

Steve Spurrier's visor slamming to the ground, Bobby Bowden's "dad gumit" phrase, Chuck Amato's hoarse voice shouting, Mark Richt's solemn seriousness with a smirk all communicate a passion about what these coaches do.

When you lead, do it with enthusiasm. If you have a passion about what you do, so will your team. Passion can be life and leadership changing. However, be careful. Passion can be destructive. If passion blinds you by taking away your balance, changing your personal goals, or affects your use of time, it can be dangerous. In his autobiography Bertrand Russell, Nobel Prize winner of Literature and a famous philosopher of the twentieth century, sought to enumerate the passions which have ruled his long life. He said:

> Three passions, simple but overwhelmingly strong, have governed my life: the longing for love, the search for knowledge, and unbearable pity for the sufferings of mankind. These passions, like great winds, have blown me hither and thither, in a wayward course, over a deep ocean of anguish, reaching to the very verge of despair.

I needed a mentor somewhere in my own life to help me understand the difference between being passionate and being driven. In the past instead of being passionate about my dreams, I allowed myself to become driven. I often wondered what my "hang-ups" were that didn't allow me to succeed as I had expected, and I even developed some theories; but the truth of the matter was that I had moved from passion to driven. I had become obsessed with "proving myself" to whomever I felt was important at that time. I had become driven to the point that I was impatient and often self-centered. That made me insensitive to other people. I was constantly striving to gain approval as opposed to living my dream, my passion. When you are passionate instead of driven, you enjoy the journey without looking for the next mountaintop.

I recall a friend asking me once, "Do you ever get enough?"

I asked, "enough of what?'

"Anything," was the way he answered.

If you are driven you never have enough of anything. You always think you can accomplish more, obtain more.

Passionate people feel deeply. However, you, as a passionate person, must be realistic in understanding that everyone does not have your passion. All the people you encounter are not climbing the same mountain you are. You don't have to make them climb with you. It is all right to be who you are, doing your own thing, even if they are not climbing with you.

Passionate people do not burnout and quit as often as driven people do. Being driven, I resigned every morning as a pastor. I would be driven to find the next goal to conquer instead of continuing my pastoring. I wonder where Coach Bowden would be if he had quit coaching when the fans burned him in effigy at West Virginia. He didn't give up. You can't steal a dream from a passionate person. Passionate people will find a way to follow their dreams even if others ignore them or try to take away their dreams.

The conclusion I have reached in this book is that you need to determine at the top of your game to be a **care-giving** leader. You, as a leader, must be a paradoxical blend of passion, humility, and commitment. You should be more like Lincoln and Socrates than Patton or Caesar. You should be ambitious, not for yourself, but for the employees of your company, the members of your team, or the people in your congregation. Decide that people matter and can be led to a point of being what or who they should be. You should:

- Set up your successors to succeed but understand that success may come long after you have gone.
- Never take yourself too seriously. Your task is always to be serious about your job but not at the expense of being cruel to others.
- See the journey as important as the destination.
- See yourself as plow-horse people, not show-horse people. Look out the windows to attribute success to factors other than yourself, but when things go poorly, look in the mirror and blame yourself and take full responsibility!

Maybe I learned that I could succeed in any endeavor that I attempted in the neighborhood where I grew up or maybe it was a part of the culture of my family. However it happened, somewhere along the way, I decided that I could accomplish my dreams if I applied myself, but that failure during the journey was all right if I learned from it.

The winners whom I have met along the way (Billy Graham, Bobby and Tommy Bowden, Charles Roesel, Mark Richt, Ken Sparks, Ed Knickman, Tim Foley, Brad Scott, Steve Cloud, the late Nick Hyder, Jimmy Scroggins, Mickey Lindsey and countless others) are not perfect, but they have set goals not only to become the best in their fields but also to use their faith to help others succeed as well. I think each keeps a list in his head, sometimes deliberately and sometimes unconsciously, that he reviews and revises at least monthly. Each list contains the information needed to reach the appropriate decision. Follow the patterns of these men. Keep a list, review it, and revise it when it becomes necessary.

When I was a little boy, I belonged to the Roy Rogers Club. It had some great rules. Maybe these rules make up the best description of a winner that exists outside of the New Testament's beatitudes. Allow me to share them with you:

Roy Rogers Riders Club Rules

1. Be neat and clean.
2. Be courteous and polite.
3. Always obey your parents.
4. Protect the weak and help them.
5. Be brave but never take chances.
6. Study hard and learn all you can.
7. Be kind to animals and take care of them.
8. Eat all your food and never waste any.
9. Love God and go to Sunday school regularly.
10. Always respect our flag and our country.

Let me close with this song written by Dale Evans Rogers that we used to sing at those meetings.

Happy Trails

Happy trails to you, until we meet again.
Happy trails to you, keep smilin' until then.
Who cares about the clouds when we're together?
Just sing a song and bring the sunny weather.
Happy trails to you, 'till we meet again.

Some trails are happy ones,
Others are blue.
It's the way you ride the trail that counts.
Here's a happy one for you.

Happy trails to you, until we meet again.
Happy trails to you, keep smilin' until then.
Who cares about the clouds when we're together?
Just sing a song and bring the sunny weather.

Happy trails to you, 'till we meet again.

Remember, it is the way you ride the trail and with whom you ride that counts. Ken agrees!

Acknowledgments

Grateful acknowledgment is made to the following sources;

Bob Biehl, *Masterplanning (The Complete Guide for Building a Strategic Plan for Your Business, Church, or Organization)*, Broadman & Holman Publishers, 1997 (800-443-1976).

Holy Bible, New Living Translation, Wheaton: Tyndale House, 1996.

Holy Bible, New International Version, Zondervan Corp., 1996.

Henry Wadsworth Longfellow, *"*Psalm of Life, *"One Hundred and One Famous Poems*, Reilly and Lee Publishers, 1958.

Dale Evans Rogers, "Happy Trails," permission granted by Roy Rogers, Jr.

Roy Rogers, "Roy Rogers Riders Club Rules," permission granted by Roy Rogers, Jr.

William Shakespeare, *Hamlet* and *Julius Caesar, Shakespeare – Revised Edition*, Hardin Craig, editor, Scott, Foresman and Company, 1958.

Ozzie Smith, July 28, 2002, Induction Speech to the National Baseball Hall of Fame, (ACME Marketing).

www.angelfire.com/hi/JeNNa/bridge2.

www.crystalinks.com/einstein.

www.fastcompany.com/online/15/one.

www.gracechurchwi.org/sermons/joshua/joshua12.

www.kanehosp.com/getpage.php?name=history.

www.search.eb.com/elections/pri/Q00062.

www./socrates.berkeley.edu/-priyas/rushdie.

www.tribute.ca/ll_actors/ios/3061.

Broadway (R) → 20th (R)
1st light Park Bar on (L)
6625 2 or 3. main Entrance
to 6th floor closs at 9P

Michael
615-595-5557